THE RED THREAD

Studies in Austrian Literature, Culture and Thought

Biography, Autobiography, Memoirs Series

Gitta Deutsch

The Red Thread

To Carol —
cordially
Gitta Deutsch

ARIADNE PRESS

Ariadne Press would like to express its appreciation to the Austrian Cultural Institute, New York and the Bundesministerium für Wissenschaft, Forschung und Kunst, Vienna for their assistance in publishing this book.

Translated from the German *Böcklinstrassenelegie*
©1993 Picus Verlag, Vienna

Library of Congress Cataloging-in-Publication Data

Deutsch, Gitta.
   [Böcklinstrassenelegie. English]
   The red thread / Gitta Deutsch.
      p.   cm. -- (Studies in Austrian literature, culture and thought. Biography, autobiography, memoirs series)
   ISBN 1-57241-019-1
   1. Deutsch, Gitta--Biography. 2. Authors, Austrian--20th century--Biography. 3. Translators--Austria--Biography.
   I. Title. II. Series: Studies in Austrian literature, culture and thought. Autobiography series.
   PT2664.E848Z46413 1996
   943.6'13004924'0092--dc20
   [B]   95-51009
                                        CIP

Cover design:
Art Director, Designer: George McGinnis

To my daughter

THE RED THREAD

Gitta Deutsch

Some years ago I realised with a shock how long it had been since I last visited the mother of my best friend at school. The old lady lived in a retirement home in Vienna's second district. We sat on her little balcony, talking only of the present. She was blind. She could not see the other side of the street, and I was glad of it. As for myself, I could not help looking across to a couple of trees where her two younger sisters had had to bury, provisionally, my friend Lotte, wrapped in a blanket.

During those last days of the war, in April

1945, there were no coffins and no transport to any cemetery. She was twenty-one when, between the air-raid shelter and her house, a grenade fragment hit her carotid artery. We had been very close for a number of reasons: our love of literature, history and the theatre, and our passionate rejection of the Nazis. My first impatient letter from England — when it was possible to write to Austria once again after the war — had been addressed to Lotte. The reply came from her mother.

When I left the home and found myself in old and familiar surroundings, I could not tear myself away. I was overwhelmed by memories. Böcklin Street, where I had spent my childhood, was steeped in summer sleepiness. Time was no longer relevant. Very little seemed to have changed. Some new blocks of flats had replaced those that were destroyed during the war, and the little wooden "Church of Our Saviour" had changed to an indifferent modern building.

Böck*lin* Street — the local intonation always lay on the second syllable, although the Swiss

painter's name was Arnold *Böck*lin. At the beginning, and on the more elegant side of our street,
there is the Academy of Art. Its walled garden,
with its sculptures, borders on the Rustenschacher-Allee where pink chestnut candles bloom
each May. And here begins the Prater — Vienna's
immense natural landscape, originally imperial
hunting grounds, which Joseph II had presented
to "his Viennese" as a gift in 1766. On the other
side of Böcklin Street — our side — are the less
elegant blocks of flats. In many of these houses
my school friends had lived, and versions of contemporary history could be written about the fate
of every one of them.

The side streets take you to Schüttel Street,
locally known as "der Schüttel," which was and is
windy, lying as it does on the Danube Canal. In
winter we used to turn up our coat collars as soon
as we reached the "Schüttel." And once again I
am pleased to see today's pretty gardens on the
banks, with their lawns and rosebushes. When I
was a child, there was only undergrowth and
stones and primitive steps leading down to an old

wooden ferry. This was pulled across on ropes, and connected the second with the third district if one did not want to walk to the nearest bridge.

As I turned around in the direction of one of these bridges, I remembered an old mill just off the street, and behind it a gardener's nursery where we used to buy lilac for Mother's Day. The last time we bought my mother lilac was in May 1937 when she was desperately ill in hospital. She cried about the lilac and the silk stockings I had brought her. The memory of it still hurts me to this day, so I pushed the thought out of my mind. I then turned back, through "our" nearest side street. At the grammar school on the corner I failed my entrance examination in mathematics when I was ten.

Opposite the school was a lending library. There I borrowed my first kitsch novels, some just permissible in the literary sense, others not. Next door to the library there was a sweet shop where you could get a great many sweets for very little money. And then there was a shop that not only sold bicycles — unrealistic even in imagination —

but it rented them by the hour or the half-hour.

There on the left is still a grocer's shop, but it no longer belongs to my old friend with the grey curls who was always full of fun. His was the first shop I was sent to alone, for there was no street to cross. He always used to present me with a large gherkin on a wooden fork, as an "extra." I do not know what became of him. I assume he shared the fate of most Jews. When I visited Vienna again for the first time in 1948, nobody would or could tell me what had happened.

One more turn and I was back again in Böcklin Street. Number twenty-six used to be the last house in a cul-de-sac, an ideal place for ballgames. Behind the wall, between Schüttel and Rustenschacher-Allee was a riding school. It is no longer there, and you can now walk through between twenty-four and twenty-six, saving a lot of time. But the old charm of number twenty-six has gone. A small door next to the main entrance leads down some steps to a carpenter's shop. When I was a child, the place used to house a Roman Catholic youth organization, and before I was of school age the Protestant child was granted a few privileges. On Corpus Christi Day I was allowed to collect a little basket of flowers, to walk in the procession and scatter the petals. Later on I was excluded from such colourful pleasures. No First Communion in a white dress and veil, holding a decorated candle, hair curled with sugar water. Nor, a few years later, the Catholic Confirmation, driving from St. Stephen's Cathedral to the Prater in a fiacre decorated with flowers, as were my Catholic friends. But the little "Church of Our Savior" between Böcklin Street and Rustenschacher-Allee was always far more homely and familiar than our Protestant Church which was a long way to go and seemed bare and austere, despite a kindly pastor who had baptised and later confirmed us.

This feeling of discrimination led me to various ways of finding substitutes. When a new bridge was opened across the Danube in 1937, we were asked at school if any of us had a white dress, white shoes, and white stockings. I put my hand up and then spent a week frantically borrowing these things in order to present the mayor with flowers. And when the time came for my Protestant Confirmation, I borrowed a Catholic godmother in the person of the much admired actress Elisabeth Kallina.

Remembering all these things, I stopped outside our house. The door was locked, but through the glass panes I could see the wide shallow steps and on each side the marble panels. In my thoughts I walked up these steps and turned left to the winding staircase, then one floor up I turned left again to the door of our flat — and to the first fourteen years of my life with all its joys and fears and sadnesses.

In May of 1937 I was taken to a children's hospital with scarlet fever. I was not very ill but terribly frightened because my mother had been in hospital for many weeks. My father had come to see me through glass doors, and then to my amazement also my aunt from Munich, and then my grandmother all dressed in black. I tried to think up comforting explanations until I noticed that my father wore a second wedding ring. I also had to stay in hospital longer than the other children for no apparent reason.

And then my father came to collect me. I asked if we could go straight to my mother for her hospital was nearby. He said something like "later" and "I must talk to you." On the way home in a taxi he began to cry — a thing I had never known him to do — and then he told me that my mother was dead. Looking now through those glass doors brought it all back again — walking up the steps arm in arm, petrified, the shock as yet stronger than the pain.

I pulled my thoughts back to the present and walked up Böcklin Street, my route to school in Wittelsbach Street which connects the Prater with a bridge across the Danube Canal. There on the left is still the Institute for the Blind; today it is a huge modern building. Opposite are the two school buildings — primary school and secondary school — and eight years of my school life. From the outside I could see no change. The high railings and behind them a few lilac bushes, the two long halls with their high windows connecting the

two schools: the gym and above it the art classroom.

I had not always been happy at school but I
was popular with my colleagues — probably because I liked to show off and was "daring." On
one occasion I even succeeded in getting a bad
mark for "behaviour," a rarity which called for a
pretend fainting fit. Our favourite school mistress
taught us German and history. I used to visit her
after the war, happy to have her call me "Gitta"
at last, and no longer "Deutsch" as the school
regulations had demanded. I was always cheeky to
our French teacher. Decades later I occasionally
met her in a café in Vienna, so I assume that she
had forgiven me.

On Wittelsbach Street I knew every shop.
There was a stationers where I spent a lot of
pocket money on photos of film stars, the bakery
with its wonderful aroma of Viennese pastries, a
chemist's strangely enough selling tiny pink,
white, or beige marshmallows. The trams used to
stop there on their way to the third and the first
districts. To save money we never used them for

short trips.

At the corner of the bridge and the "Schüttel" there used to be a Christmas tree market. On dark winter mornings, on my way to school, it was worth the detour along the Schüttel to pick up fir or spruce twigs for decoration at home or in the classroom. Nobody minded and the country sellers who warmed their hands by their paraffin lamps were a great deal friendlier than the caretaker in our house, the school warden, or the local pub keepers, who used to terrify us by their sudden "What do you think you're doing?" when one just happened to pick a twig of lilac in the schoolyard or a few ivy leaves from a pub garden. The caretaker at our house used to spy on us through a hole in his door to make sure we had wiped our shoes on the mat.

I now walked back again along the Schüttel. At the next corner there still is a small restaurant, not the one I remember from the rare occasions I was taken there by my parents. I loved the boiled beef on its traditional oval dish surrounded by doll's portions of different vegetables. A little further on there used to be a greengrocer's, kept by an elderly Jewish couple — but they of course have gone. My mother was fond of them, and I was always given a forkful of sauerkraut on a piece of paper. I do not know what became of them, and once again, as so often, I felt the great bitterness swelling up, unchanged since 1938.

* * *

On my return home I searched among the books of my late father to see if I could find a publication on Vienna's second district, the "Leopoldstadt." Here again the Viennese have their own intonation by stressing the third rather than the first syllable, as they would with the name Leopold. I found such a book. It had been published in Vienna in 1937. On the title page I found scribbled in my father's minute scholarly hand the laconic words: "Prohibited in 1938" and underneath: "Bought in 1939." I began to turn the pages, and under the heading "Böcklinstrasse" I read a note of his in the margin: "OED — No. 26 = 1919–39" — his initials, the number of our house, and the years he had spent there. He must have bought this book secondhand in his last year in Vienna before he fled to Britain.

The book was published "privately by the Teachers' Association of the Second District," and one of the names seemed familiar: Hans Schedling. Strange how the threads seem to cross! I remembered a class photo taken in 1933, and when I found it I discovered that on the back I had as a nine-year-old written the names of all the girls and added "Class Mistress: Spiro" and "Headmaster: Dir. H. Schedling."

Until 1919 Böcklin Street had been called Valerie Street, after Emperor Francis Joseph's younger daughter. And that was the year my parents moved there.

* * *

My father's parents came from Nikolsburg (today's Mikulov) in Moravia. At that time it was part of Austria, and my grandparents belonged to the large German-speaking Jewish community there. It is said that my great-grandfather Deutsch ran a removal firm with a horse and cart. I only know my grandfather Ignaz Deutsch from an old photograph. He is sitting on a wickerwork chair, his hat on his knees, a cigar in his mouth, and with a part roguish, part embarrassed smile. He had moved to Vienna as a young man and founded a small firm that sold brass and copper rods and pipes. Later on the family lived on the first floor. But for the time being he was a bachelor and worked so hard that when he was "recommended" a wife in Nikolsburg, he could only spare an afternoon to get to know her. He took a train to Nikolsburg, and Ernestine Gewitsch met him at the station. They went for a walk and discussed the essentials. As far as I know, it turned out to be a good marriage blessed with three sons and two daughters.

It is said that my grandfather used to take a regular midmorning break in a pub across the way, where he ate a goulash and smoked a Virginia cigar. On his way there he passed a tobacconist's and always bought a national-lottery coupon. And then one day he hit the jackpot. The lion's share was naturally invested in the firm. But my grandmother also had a share, and with it she gratified what must have been her great desire: she installed painted windows displaying all Grimm's fairy tales. I well remember those windows that made the living room rather dark, for this was where she presided over the family tea parties. She died when I was six. Half a century later I found my grandparents' grave in the old Jewish part of Vienna's largest cemetery. Like most of them, it was completely overgrown.

But to return to my father's childhood. Between May and October my grandparents used to rent a furnished flat "in the country" — in their case this was Baden, now about forty minutes from Vienna. It was customary to take the family maid, crockery, pots and pans, and bed linen. The name Deutsch can be read in the visitors' lists of the small town. While the children were at school, they travelled to Vienna every morning and returned in the afternoon. And my grandfather presumably went to his office in Vienna throughout those five months. In those days the tram between Vienna and Baden was steam-driven, although in later years it became one of the first electric inter-urban trams. The oddity of the rails being laid alternatively on the left or the right side of the road is due to the fact that for each part of the track the cheaper piece of land had been bought.

My father, Otto Deutsch — as a young writer he later added the second name Erich — was the youngest of five brothers and sisters. While he was still at school he began to write newspaper articles. He converted to the Protestant faith as a young man without ever disowning his Jewish origin. He was not a religious man but — as he used to say — he regarded every religion as "a formula for a decent life." He had studied history of art and history of literature at the universities of Vienna and Graz, and was about to write a thesis on the Austrian painter Moritz von Schwind when he discovered Franz Schubert. Schwind belonged to that interesting and artistic circle of friends around Schubert. OED (Otto Erich Deutsch) was so fascinated by Schubert that he switched his studies to the history of music.

He was already on the way to his future work and research. As early as 1905 he published his first book about the composer, a little volume entitled *Schubert–Brevier*.

In 1908 and 1909 he was an art critic for the Vienna daily paper *Die Zeit,* and for two years served as an assistant lecturer at the Institute of History of Art at the University of Vienna. He had already written nearly thirty books and articles on Schubert when he published *Franz Schubert — His Life in Pictures* in 1913, and the first version of his *Franz Schubert — The Documents of His Life* in 1914. He spent the First World War as a cavalry officer in the Austro-Hungarian army in Northern Italy. He kept a horse, a hen, a canary, and a rather dim dog who suffered an untimely end after eating drawing-pins.

After the war, OED bought the bookshop Seidel & Sohn on the Graben in the centre of Vienna and integrated it with a small publishing firm that brought typically Austrian books. He took on a young trainee named Rudolf Bing who, as Sir Rudolf, later became director of the New York Metropolitan Opera. OED was no businessman, however, and the bookshop did not survive for long.

Between 1926 and 1935 he was employed as librarian by the wealthy Dutch music collector Anthony van Hoboken, whose catalogue of Haydn's compositions is said to owe quite a bit to my father's work. My mother, who had been a friend of Hoboken's first wife, was rash and loyal enough to defend her at a party in the presence of the second Mrs. van Hoboken. One day later my father lost his job, and that was a severe blow to our family finances. I can still remember my mother crying at my bedside and telling me that we would have to economise more than ever.

In 1930 and 1931 OED published a periodical called *Die Freyung,* with contributors like the author Otto Stoessl and the composer Ernst Krenek. He also became a freelance writer, and — until 1938 — music critic for the Swiss *Basler Nationalzeitung.*

* * *

My mother's family came from South Germany. My great-grandfather Dr. Adolf Richter was professor of chemistry and vice-president of the German Peace League. A street and a bridge in Pforzheim are named after him. His cousin Eugen Richter was at the head of the German Progressive Party and is said to have had many a fierce argument with the current Parliamentary President Eduard von Simson. Generations later my daughter married a descendant of Eduard von Simson, with the amusing result that the two warring politicians are now united in my granddaughter Juliet.

Going back further, the men in the Richter generations alternated as Protestant parsons and doctors. One of them made a name for himself as an army doctor in Beresina during the Napoleonic Wars.

My great-grandfather Müller was stationmaster in Ulm on the Danube. He had a large family, and one of his daughters went to England and became a housekeeper. She married a German who was interned on the Isle of Man during the

First World War. When I came to England in 1938, she was a newly discovered relative, and I used to visit the old lady in her little terrace house in Kilburn. I loved her German sauerbraten — marinated roast beef. Her very English son Will tried in vain to teach me how to dissect a smoked kipper. He did not speak a word of German, whereas my great-aunt managed to speak English with a Swabian accent!

My grandfather Wilhelm Müller moved to Pforzheim as a young man and became an apprentice in one of the town's many factories producing artificial jewellery. He must have been very gifted and hard-working because he succeeded in setting up his own factory. Such careers within one generation were by no means uncommon in the nineteenth century. He married Jenny Richter but died before he was fifty, leaving a relatively young widow with four children. I did not know this grandfather either, but we visited my grandmother in the Black Forest every other summer. After her husband's death she wore only brown, grey, or dark blue, always with a velvet ribbon around her neck. Her marriage had not been very happy, and this may have been the paradoxical reason for her puritanical attitude toward her long widowhood.

The Müller brothers and sisters were exceptionally tall. This was a depressing problem for the two sisters throughout their lives. My mother could afford only ready-made shoes, so she had to buy men's shoes; women's were not made in her size. It was easier for the two brothers, although the younger was almost seven feet, and as children we regarded him with a certain shy reverence.

My mother, Hanna, was the eldest and already grown up when her father died. She was beautiful and had inherited his sunny nature. I have photos of her when she was young, at the piano, skiing, or dressed as Joan of Arc at her Swiss finishing school, and as a Red Cross nurse with colleagues, doctors, and patients — at least a head taller than anyone else and always full of fun.

Her friends called her "die schöne Müllerin," partly because her father bore the identical name to the poet of Schubert's famous "Müller-Lieder."

And she was game for anything.

When the First World War broke out, she registered as a nurse with the Austrian Red Cross because it was said that they would even send their nurses to the front, unlike the German Red Cross. She was soon in charge of a field hospital, and when the front drew nearer, she decided to evacuate the wounded. She had two horses harnessed to a farm cart, her patients were laid on it, and she herself drove the horses at great speed through the front lines. After several such excursions they were all safe, and as one of only two women, she was awarded two medals for outstanding courage.

The war was still on when she met Otto Erich Deutsch. He had arrived in her field hospital loaded with a pile of books, and her first words to him were "And who do you think you are?" But like so many women she fell for the charm of the unheroic Viennese intellectual, and they were married in Pforzheim in 1917, much to the disapproval of "Grandmère Jenny," as my cousin Micha calls our mutual grandmother.

When the war was over, my parents moved to Vienna and soon to the flat in Böcklin Street. Her husband's family warmly welcomed the young woman. Her special ways were a great success in Vienna. Despite all her efforts to learn certain Viennese tongue twisters, she retained her Swabian intonation, and only her relatives in the Black Forest claimed that she spoke Viennese.

* * *

The flat in Böcklin Street was large by Viennese standards. The rent was controlled, but even so my parents found it expensive.

My brother Peter was born in 1920, and I in 1924. We grew up in a liberal, rather unpolitical middle-class milieu, with a very Austria-conscious father and our humourous and warmhearted mother from the Black Forest. She was the calming influence in our lives, beloved and popular with people of all social classes. None of us ever really got over her early death. My cousin Micha told me that, as a little boy at their very first encounter, he had "thrown his heart into her arms!"

I sometimes dream of her and that I met her again as a very old woman. And in my dreams I reproach her for not having come back: "If you were alive all that time . . . ." She was buried in June 1937 on the outskirts of Vienna, on a hill in the wine-growing region, while I was still in hospital with scarlet fever. Later, when we had to leave Austria, my father had her coffin cremated and the urn sent to her family's grave in Pforzheim, where all the Richters and Müllers are buried. It is a large plot, overgrown with ivy, and behind it stands the stone figure of a wayfarer with the inscription "Lord, stay with us, for the evening is near." On our visits to the Black Forest my mother always picked an ivy leaf from the grave and put it in her wallet.

During Advent she insisted on making ten different kinds of Christmas pastry: the same ten recipes that her sister used in Munich and her mother in the Black Forest. Nevertheless, the three women always sent each other samples of those identical biscuits. They usually arrived rather the worse for their postal journey.

My grandmother on the other hand had a habit of knitting bed socks year after year: beige for my father, white for my mother, pale blue for Peter, and pink for me. We must have had drawers full of bed socks, just as my poor father must have had drawers full of the "pulse-warmers" I knitted every year for his birthday.

In summer my parents used to rent a furnished flat somewhere in the country. We would stay four to six weeks, with my father joining us for the weekend. The rest of the week he would spend in Vienna or at the Salzburg Festival writing music reviews. I think he rather enjoyed these bachelor periods.

Among my holiday memories I treasure two summers we spent at Seewalchen am Attersee, in a house by the lake. There are some lovely paintings by Gustav Klimt of "Schloss Kammer," a yellow castle with an avenue of trees which we could see from our house. There were birthday parties for my brother with wild strawberries and whipped cream, photos of the many children we played with, or of my parents dressed up for a fancy-dress party.

Two or three summers we spent in Trofaiach in Styria. There again I retain a mental kaleidoscope of memories: a photo with both my brothers — our older Italian half-brother spent his holidays with us — myself in T-shirt and leather shorts. At an inn where we used to eat our lunch — the main meal of the day — to my delight the soup was still poured into the plates from metal cups. The innkeeper, Frau Blaschke, and her recipes are immortalised in my mother's handwritten cookery book. This book has sentimental value for it contains handwritings of us all. Apart from my mother's, some recipes were copied by Peter and myself, and the index was written by my father. Trofaiach spells forest honey for breakfast, salads bought from a convent garden, and a favorite red dirndl with a pattern of white garden rakes. It is strange how one remembers the feel and even the colour of a dress just by looking at a black and white photograph. At a nearby swimming pool I inadvertently learned to swim when someone pushed me into the water.

Every other summer we travelled to Germany with my mother. We usually spent a few nights with our relatives in Munich to break the long journey to Neuenbürg on the river Enz. As soon as we reached the first Black Forest fir trees, my mother would call out: "Breathe in deeply, children!" Neuenbürg was a paradise for us and our Munich cousins. If we adhered to the strict rules of Grandmère Jenny or kept out of her way, our holidays there had a lot to offer. The large garden was laid out on three levels. When I saw it again some years after the war, it seemed a lot smaller, the way most things do once you are grown up. On the lowest level, by the street, there was a little garden house. One summer my cousin Tis and I decorated it with little paper flags for an uncle's birthday. At that time in Germany, in 1935, you could buy only black-white-red or swastika flags. After the party we shared these flags. I left the swastika flags to my cousin, with a depreciating remark, and then stuck strips of red paper over the black, so as to have the Austrian colors of red-white-red. The result of all this was a patriotic row during which we rubbed sand into each other's freshly washed hair.

My grandmother's house was on the second level, and some distance away stood a wooden hut that was used as an overflow for guests. In front of it grew an old apple tree, and one of the Richter cousins — whom I hero-worshipped — deposited me on one of its branches when I became tiresome one day. He even took a snapshot of my misery before he walked away.

On the top level were the vegetable garden and all kinds of berries. Further up there was a little iron gate that led to the woods, where we picked blueberries and mushrooms. My grandmother was an excellent cook; she produced things we loved but were not used to, and they all had different names in Germany. In her cellar she kept runner-beans preserved in salt in huge earthenware pots; she made numerous jams, and sweetsour cucumbers, vegetable marrow slices, and plums to be served with meat.

For breakfast there were fresh rolls called "Laugeweck" and butter. Those of us who were up early were allowed to go to the village with a wooden handcart to collect chunks of ice wrapped in sackcloth for the icebox and fresh "Laugeweck." These rolls were brushed with a salty brine before they were baked, and they do not taste nearly as good anywhere else.

In the summer of 1935 my mother had to have a special permit to take her "half-Jewish" daughter to Hitler-Germany. She always voiced her political opinions very openly, and she would have endangered herself considerably if she had done this in Vienna in 1938. As it happened, the occasion did not arise. She died at the age of forty-four in 1937 — one year before Hitler marched into Austria — of streptococcal infection, an illness which ten years later could have been cured with the discovery of penicillin.

Part of my school holidays were spent with childless relatives on my father's side in Reichenau in Lower Austria, in a beautiful house near the Hotel Thalhof, owned at one time by one of Arthur Schnitzler's great loves.

My uncle used to take the dog and me for a

walk around the garden before breakfast. From the top terrace we could watch the little local train go by. Lower down he would inspect his beloved black currants, and on the lowest level underneath the trees grew masses of the delicate scented wild cyclamens long before the time when they had to be listed for environmental protection. The dog — a schnauzer — and I had something in common: one of us, or both, were bound to be sick in the car, and bets were made on which would be first! Reichenau also has its culinary memories for me: apricot dumplings in butter and grated gingerbread, not just bread crumbs, and far too many trout: my uncle, alas, was a passionate angler. At times it seemed to me that breakfast was the only meal without trout being served one way or another.

During the last summer of my mother's life, I was in Reichenau with her. In fact we had the house to ourselves because the owners had gone away. We asked three peasant children to stay and really spoiled them. They had a wonderful holiday. When our relatives returned earlier than expected they found my unconventional mother and me dancing to gramophone music with the gardener and the cook.

My parents' life in Vienna in the twenties and thirties was always overshadowed by money worries, and yet we led a relatively comfortable life. Invitations to meals were issued rarely, but it was usual to ask friends in for coffee after meals, and my parents had an interesting circle of friends: writers, painters, actors, and scholars.

When I was a child, we had a governess at first and a cook. When we could no longer afford them, they were able to "step up" in life quite considerably. Maria became lady's maid to the wife of an adjutant to the King of England and lived at St. James's Palace until the outbreak of war. And our Poldi, the cook, became a children's nurse and later assistant in a doctor's surgery.

My father was separated from us children behind upholstered doors, and we often saw him only at mealtimes. He liked working at night, with a thermos flask of black coffee by his side. He used to take me to museums and exhibitions, or help me — unsuccessfully — with my maths homework. But it was our mother who dealt with our everyday problems. I used to go shopping with her and, if I had done well at school, she would treat me to a gateau at one of the best cake-shops. We also went to the pictures together. To Charlie Chaplin and Shirley Temple, and to her particular love, Greta Garbo. I did not share her interest in football but I know she liked to go to all the big matches.

My brother, four years older than I, had his own friends and interests. But we shared our love for the nearby "Wurstelprater" — amusement park would be a poor description for it. He had good connections there and was allowed to help out with the "live horses." They were called that to differentiate them from the wooden merry-go-round horses. Sometimes he would let me ride on a pony, with the understanding that I would not disgrace him by revealing that I was his little sister. That would have embarrassed him. During those days he developed his later passion for riding, a sport that our family finances did not stretch to.

The remaining huge "Prater" area was our playground. In the winter we would toboggan, in the summer play hide-and-seek and other games. My mother would take a folding chair and a basket full of socks to darn. On the long main Prater avenue with its 12,000 white blossoming chestnut trees, you could ride on rented bicycles. In May there was a procession of flower-decorated cars and carriages; in the summer various aunts would take us to the coffeehouse on *Konstantinhügel* — an artificial hill consisting of the earth that had to be dug up when the *Rotunde* trade fair building was erected. And like the children in other parts of the world, we collected the beautiful shiny chestnuts in autumn. But the most wonderful events in Vienna were visits to the *Burgtheater* and, a little later, the opera house.

In two consecutive years I was allowed to act in a children's play myself. The big parts were played by professionals, and the smaller parts by children. I was a snowdrop in the first act and when the curtain went up I had to say the first words — something like "I hear a singing and a ringing that comes to us from far away." To which a gentian replied: "I can't hear anything and I'm not deaf!" The audience laughed and clapped: they had not heard me either! In the second act I lost some of my shyness and became more audible as a cyclamen in a beautiful silk and velvet cyclamen-coloured dirndl.

For a very short time I learned to play the piano but without success. I got as far as Don Giovanni's easy champagne aria, and that was the end of my musical career. I was equally hopeless at sports. As a city child I was sent out to get "fresh air" as often as possible. There was an ice-skating rink near us but, as I frequently fell down, I spent more time by the smoking stove in the cloakroom drying out than on the ice in the fresh air.

At school I was the worst girl at gym but the best in German. I was often asked to recite poetry or to read my essays aloud, and these were welcome occasions to show off my acting talents.

As often as our pocket money would allow,

my friends and I bought tickets for the top gallery of the Burgtheater. We knew Schiller's *Don Carlos* by heart and cried our eyes out over Romeo and Juliet. After each performance we raced down the four flights of stairs to the stage door, where a crowd of young people gathered to see their revered actors and actresses "in the flesh" as it were, asking for autographs and telling them how wonderful they were. Fred Liewehr, the handsome hero of the classical repertoire, retained his sense of humour when we laid flowers on the roof of his car or chalked LONG LIVE DON CARLOS! LONG LIVE LIEWEHR! on the pavements.

One little anecdote illustrates our childish enthusiasm. Three of us had discovered where Liewehr lived and had got as far as the door to his flat in the hope of collecting something as a souvenir. The only thing that was removable was his doormat. We walked around St. Stephen's Cathedral with it a couple of times, trying to decide what to do with the wretched thing. None of us had the courage to take it home in one piece, and it was too thick to cut into three. So we very sheepishly returned the trophy, hoping fervently that we would not meet our hero on the stairs.

Life was interesting and fairly unburdened when we were children. I am afraid we did not ask ourselves how our mother managed it all. Some years ago I came across a letter she had written to her sister: "I really don't know how I am to provide Christmas presents for the children this year. . . ." She always made it possible. She economised — mainly on herself. She taught herself to make attractive silk scarves from remnants cut on the bias and sold them to her friends. She often sat at her sewing machine late at night when all her other tasks were done.

The twenties and thirties were a time of poverty and unemployment in Austria as in other parts of Europe. We kept a plate with small coins in our hall for the many beggars who knocked on the door, or for the musicians playing in the street. People often came to the door asking for bread or a plateful of warm food. When I was at elementary school, the poorest children came early and were given hot cocoa and bread before the classes started. This was done discreetly but the children concerned felt stigmatised nevertheless. There was always a Christmas tree in the gym hall with presents for the poorest provided anonymously by those whose parents could afford it.

We also had to economise at home. Dresses and coats were let down or turned inside out more than once, and it was never considered embarrassing to pass on or accept clothes that we or others had grown out of. Several times a year a seamstress came to spend the day with us to mend the bed linen.

* * *

Once again I picked up my father's book about the Leopoldstadt district, searching for chronological details during my childhood. Some I remembered, others I discovered only from this book.

The year of my birth, 1924, saw the introduction of the new Austrian currency, the Schilling, and Austrian radio broadcast its first programme. As early as 1925 there were clashes between National Socialists and Social Democrats, and the illegal Austrian Hitler movement was founded. In the same year, on the other hand, the municipality of "Red Vienna" had erected the 25,000th workers' flat in the famous *Karl-Marx-Hof.*

In 1927, when I was three, two demonstrators — an invalid and a child — were shot by right-wing extremists in the village of Schattendorf in the eastern province of Burgenland. The murderers were acquitted. The workers' anger sparked off a general strike, and the government set armed mounted police against them. The Ministry of Justice was set on fire. Laconically, the book records: "Five policemen killed, and eighty-six demonstrators."

The year 1928 marked the hundredth anniversary of Schubert's death. Apart from numerous concerts and ceremonies, there were endless manifestations of kitsch. Schubert postcards, stamps, matchboxes, chocolate boxes with his picture, Schubert made of soap and even of lard! Schubert with the fictitious *Dreimäderlhaus,* the three sisters that never existed but were linked with his name in the equally fictitious operetta "Lilac Time." My four-year-old childish comment is said to have been that I was "sick and tired of Schubert."

The winter of 1928–1929 was bitterly cold and brought great hardship to the poor. Huge blocks of ice were floating on the Danube, and some of the time you could walk across the river. I seem to remember similar ice blocks on our nearby Danube Canal. From the roof of our house we marvelled at one of the first cigar-shaped Zeppelins flying over Vienna.

I noted that in 1930 the first International Women's Congress was taking place in Vienna. And I, as a six-year-old, started school in September. I learned my first lesson in wisdom: each child was allowed to pick a wrapped parcel from a laundry basket, and the large one I grabbed turned out to be a frame with wooden beads on wire to teach one to count. My lifelong disturbed relationship to numbers may well go back to that early experience!

What seemed to me the most interesting occurrence in 1931 — due, no doubt, to my great sympathy for the man — was Albert Einstein's visit to Vienna. Dollfuss became Austria's Federal Chancellor in 1932. Yet the 29th World Peace Congress was held in Vienna!

By 1933 the Austrian Parliament had been eliminated — that was the beginning of authoritarian government. The death penalty was brought back. And in Germany Adolf Hitler came to power.

On 12 February 1934 a general strike was called in Vienna. Government troops fired on workers' flats in the Karl-Marx-Hof and the Goethe-Hof. There were many casualties. A corporate state was proclaimed. It was Austro-Fascism at its height. And yet in the same year, in July, four Nazi thugs entered the chancellery and murdered Dollfuss.

The general rearmament that took place in Europe in 1935 had not penetrated my childhood awareness any more than the Spanish Civil War which broke out in 1936. Hitler supported Franco

and his Fascists. It was his "dress rehearsal" for
the Second World War, which he started three
years later. Many young Austrian volunteers
fought against Franco, side by side with other
young Europeans.

Our Christmas in 1936 was the same as ever
— and yet different. It was family tradition that
we go for a walk and not return until we had seen
three lighted Christmas trees. It kept us out of the
way while our mother decorated our tree, and
only when she called us were we allowed into the
dining room. She would sit at the piano playing
"Silent Night." The electric light was out, and
only the candles were burning. Only after the
third verse of "Silent Night" were we allowed to
start unwrapping presents. Somewhere during the
third verse I seem to remember hearing a soft
meow emanating from a little pink-lined basket.
It was also the Christmas when one of us had the
silly idea of suggesting that each of us choose a
candle to see which would last longest. As it
happened, my mother's went out first. She died
the following June — and this proved to be my

most painful personal experience for many decades to come.

On 17 September 1937 the Rotunde — the huge exhibition hall in the Prater — burned down. We also watched this event from the roof of our house. People referred to it as a bad omen, and the same was said the following January when the northern nights (aurora borealis) were seen over Vienna.

* * *

The seriousness of the first months of 1938 overshadowed our life at school. We had been aware of events for a long time and talked of nothing but politics. There was fear but also a new, spontaneous patriotism. "Austria" had become our motto.

A plebiscite was arranged for 13 March. It was to demonstrate to Hitler that Austria wished to remain independent. But it was too late. The various anti-Nazi groups had failed to unite in time.

As yet, our class was divided into two political sides. The Nazi sympathisers openly welcomed the pending "Anschluss" with Germany. They had long been wearing white knee-length socks — one of the Nazi symbols. The rest of us fought with passionate speeches and leaflets. In the inner city, daily demonstrations and counter-demonstrations took place, usually degenerating into fights. I was often and secretly in the middle of such scenes, with all the reckless abandon of a fourteen-year-old.

On 11 March Schuschnigg, the Federal Chancellor, made his last statement on the radio. Hitler's ultimatum to him meant the end of Austria. My father and I were listening to it together, and then he telephoned the Swiss newspaper whose music critic he was. It was his only political report and it almost cost him his life.

To forestall the Austrian plebiscite fixed for 13 March, Hitler sent his troops across the border the day before. Pictures of cheering crowds were shown around the world as a sign of the Austrians' full agreement with the Anschluss. These scenes of fanatical enthusiasm did indeed take place and cannot be denied. But it is not the entire story. Within the next six weeks between 50,000 and 76,000 Austrians were arrested. And no pictures exist of the despair that took place behind closed doors, no record of the hundreds of suicides within the first few days.

The schools were closed for a week in March 1938. Austria had been degraded to the name "Ostmark" — a province of the "Great German Reich." My friend Lotte and I borrowed what we could in the way of black clothes to wear on the first day after school reopened. "We mourn for Austria," we told those who had already turned up in Hitler Youth uniforms. Our needlework teacher was in tears when she saw me: "I am so terribly sorry that you're not an Aryan!"

"Aryan" I was certainly not but, according to Hitler's racial laws, a "first degree half-breed." That meant that I had fifty percent "Jewish blood" in my veins. Before our lessons we no longer prayed but were expected to stretch out our right hands at a certain angle and cry "Heil Hitler!" Those of us who were in passive resistance remained seated and silent during the Nazi songs that any child could demand to be sung in the middle of any lesson. The teachers knew better than to oppose the "good Nazis" who could and would denounce them. Opposition would have cost them their jobs or worse. I have been asked why or how we had such pluck in those early days, and I can only think that it was foolhardiness and inexperience, for we very soon learned to keep our opinions to ourselves

— certainly when we heard of the horrors of mass arrests and brutalities. People were hauled out of their homes and forced to scrub the pavements. Old men and women were handed pails and brushes and sometimes, for the amusement of particularly sadistic audiences, even toothbrushes!

There was a girl in my class who looked like her Jewish father, and yet her mother swore an official oath that she was not his daughter. I was quite horrified. The Jewish girls were sent to another, purely Jewish, school. I asked if I could join them and was not allowed to, owing to my fifty percent "non-Jewish blood!"

I wondered where so many swastika flags came

from in such a short time. People one had known for years looked the other way when one met them on the street.

My friends and I still went to the Burgtheater, on cheap tickets, and there we sat on the fourth gallery when they played Schiller's *Don Carlos,* with Goebbels, the German propaganda minister, lording it in the centre box known as the "Emperor's." At the Marquis of Posa's famous "Sire, give us freedom of thought!" we clapped so enthusiastically that the rest of the audience joined in — before the usher threw us out.

The Burgtheater was still an unclouded joy, and some of us hoped one day to be accepted at the "Max Reinhardt Seminar" drama school. Through my godmother I managed to persuade the Burgtheater actor Heinz Woester to test my talent. With angelic patience he listened and watched me do scenes from *Romeo and Juliet,* Shaw's *St. Joan,* Kleist's *Käthchen von Heilbronn* and Hauptmann's *Versunkene Glocke* At the end he simply said: "A great deal of feeling. Too much!"

My uncertain talent was never seriously put to the test. The Reinhardt Seminar would have been out of reach for me under Hitler, and later in England I did not get past the amateur stage.

I was great friends with a Jewish classmate of my brother's, a gentle, sensitive boy four years older than myself. We both wrote poetry, we read plays together, or met for serious talks in the park after school. There we could not even sit down — the words FOR ARYANS ONLY being printed on all the benches. One afternoon he did not turn up at the usual time. Nazi thugs in uniform had hung a placard around his neck reading DON'T BUY FROM JEWS! and forced him to walk up and down a bridge for many hours. Soon after that he fled to Trieste and later to what was then Palestine, and we only met again in Vienna forty years later.

Despite all the horrors and anxieties, it was a beautiful spring, and at fourteen one is easily diverted. I was in love with Vienna — yes, even with the terrible Vienna of 1938. Nature had remained unchanged, the chestnuts on the Prater's

main avenue were in white blossom, those in our
Rustenschacher-Allee in pink. The scent of lilac
was the same as in other years. In May I was confirmed.

My school days ended in June. A photo of my
class — already without the "100% Jewish" girls
— is very significant, now that I look at it again.
At the time I wrote all the names on the back of
the photograph. With only four exceptions I had
scribbled one or two swastikas above each name
— one for mere supporters and two for the pre–
1938 Nazis. The four "good Austrians" were of
course my friend Lotte Repa and I, gentle Hansi
Popp, and Gretl Hafner, half-Jewish like myself
and, unlike myself, a sports genius. She won every
competition in ice skating and swimming and
greatly impressed me with her "otherness."

Our form mistress had no option but to toe
the line, though in our eyes she had remained
decent. Our new headmaster had been in prison
as an illegal Nazi until the "Anschluss" and was
then straightaway appointed to our school.
Strangely enough he was interested in me and

kept asking me to his office for coffee. When on one occasion he came too close, I was so horrified that I spilled my coffee over his suit. Despite this incident he wrote me a very positive and flattering letter of recommendation addressed to my future school in England.

In July I was sent to a Hungarian family on Lake Balaton. They wanted their two daughters to speak German for a few weeks. Again I managed to forget our political troubles for a while. I loved swimming in the lake and learned to dance the Csardas. After that I spent a few days in Budapest with relatives, who spoiled me with presents and new clothes.

In the meantime, however, my family in Vienna had decided that I must be sent to England through the Quakers' Children's Committee. There were still several months during which I was to learn "something useful." I joined a dressmaking course but was very soon thrown out for lack of membership in a Nazi organisation. The English lessons I was meant to attend privately were boring. On my way there I preferred to get out of the tram and walk up a little footpath to Sievering cemetery where my mother was buried.

Early in November Vienna, too, had its *Reichskristallnacht* — the "crystal" cynically referred to the broken glass in shop windows and synagogues. A German diplomat had been shot in Paris by a seventeen-year-old Jewish boy whose family had been deported, and the Nazi authorities had as a result not only permitted acts of violence but actually encouraged them. Synagogues were set on fire, Jewish shops looted, and people dragged out of their homes and beaten up. My cousin Stephan was arrested in the street and sent to the Dachau concentration camp.

A few days later four men knocked at our door. They were not in uniform, just wearing swastika armbands. One of them was our local coal merchant. They had come, they said, to "search Jewish homes for arms!" In a cupboard in the hall they actually came across an old sabre from the First World War. When they wanted to take my father, I ran out on the landing and started to scream. A few of the more courageous neighbours came out and protested against such an "illegal arrest of a respectable tenant" — and the four men left sheepishly with the remark: "He's a harmless Jew anyhow!"

* * *

On 27 November the time had come for me to leave Vienna. I was wearing a new navy blue coat and hat and what the family had considered as "English" clothes. We were not allowed to take out valuables or money except ten German *Reichsmarks.* Later it was still possible for an aunt to send me her entire collection of Goethe, Schiller, Lessing, and Shakespeare — it was the last I heard of her. A few years later she was arrested from her hiding place in Budapest and deported to the Theresienstadt concentration camp. On that late November day I wore under my blouse a narrow velvet ribbon with a glass medallion and in it was a red thread pulled from a seat in the Burgtheater on my last visit. And in my purse, next to the permitted ten *Reichsmarks,* there was a tiny bit of stone from the wall of St. Stephen's Cathedral.

In the autumn of 1993 my daughter discovered the red thread in an old copy of the *Oxford Book of English Verse* which I must have given to her when she was still at school. I was convinced that I had lost that thread decades ago.

Two of my girl friends had come to see me off at the bus that was to take me to the small airport at Aspern. We promised to meet at the Polish sandwich bar in Dorotheer Street "the day after Hitler's death." One friend stayed in Vienna — her parents had gone ahead into French exile and were murdered by the Nazis after the German invasion. The other fled to the United States, and when she visited Vienna forty-five years later, she showed her grown-up children the rooms — offices today — where she and her sister had slept as girls. And I was to spend the next thirty-one years in England.

So on this 27th of November I flew to London on my own. In those days one had to change planes three times. The first time in Munich, where my "Aryan" grandmother met me, embarrassingly with an unwrapped toy dog which I

quickly gave away in the next plane. My grandmother reminded me that I was a "German girl"!
That was all I needed. Furiously I told her that I
was Austrian and half-Jewish, and that this was
the reason I was being sent to England. It was my
last encounter with Grandmère Jenny, and so we
remained unpleasantly in each other's memory.
The next plane landed in Cologne where one of
my mother's school friends fondly embraced me,
and when I reached the Brussels airport in the
third plane, I was greeted by a friend of my
father's. The last and Belgian plane was small and
the flight bumpy, so that the stretch across the
British Channel added airsickness to my fears and
agitations.

   After more than half a century all these details
of my first fourteen years make up a mosaic that
I wanted to preserve, not only for myself but for
the younger and youngest generations. We are all
part of such a mosaic, consisting of our own
experiences, but also of the experiences of others.
Although those years can be said to have treated
me far more gently than so many others, I still

belong to the period and to its suffering. The nightmare of 1938 to 1945 is deeply rooted in me. Here again, as so often, words of the Austrian poet Erich Fried in his poem "Against Forgetting" seem to express all this better than I can. Translated it reads:

> I want to remember
> that I do not want to forget
> for I want to be myself
> I want to remember
> that I want to forget
> for I do not want to suffer so
> much
>
> I want to remember
> that I do not want to forget
> that I want to forget
> for I want to know myself
>
> for I cannot think
> without remembering
> for I cannot wish
> without remembering
> for I cannot love

for I cannot hope
for I cannot forget
without remembering

I want to remember
everything one forgets
for without remembering
I cannot save
either myself or my children . . .

* * *

The Belgian plane landed at the small British airport of Croydon, and there I was met by my former governess. She brought me to the home of some distant relatives where I spent the night. They "showed me London" the next day — I remember only Buckingham Palace and Harrods' store — and in the afternoon I was handed over to my English Quaker hostess at Victoria Station. In the train I sat opposite a cool and reserved lady whose German was as bad as my English, and we travelled to a south coast town. I remember thinking that this complete extradition of my person was reminiscent of what happened to the fifteen-year-old Archduchess Marie Antoinette. At the French border the future Dauphine of France not only had to leave behind her companions and her language, but she also had to exchange her Austrian clothes for French ones in a specially erected tent. I felt that from now on everything would be new and strange and different for me as well. I could not feel any gratitude for being saved, and the homesickness of those first days never left me entirely in thirty-one years.

My hosts lived in a large house with a garden. They had five children, all younger than myself. There was a children's nurse in that in-between situation of being neither servant nor family. I had my suppers with her in the day-nursery after the younger children had gone to bed. Husband and wife dined alone in evening dress and dinner jacket. The nurse disliked me from the first day and considered me an intruder.

The other employees consisted of a Jewish cook from Vienna, not a real cook but someone who, as a refugee, could get a work permit only for domestic service; then there were two housemaids of my own age, wearing uniform and working hard and long hours. They all slept in unheated attics and spent their free time below stairs. I was not allowed to make friends with any of them. Of course I talked to the Viennese cook and the two girls until the trouble-making nurse found out and told my hostess.

I was given a pretty little room but felt very lonely. The younger children found me comical, and there was giggling and whispering when they saw me. They went to a different school; I had been granted a place that was open in the local grammar school. To my horror we had to wear uniform — a white flannel blouse with a navy blue tunic, thick grey stockings, and black shoes. And with it a round black felt hat which could in no way be worn at an attractive angle. Even our underwear was part of the uniform. Once a week I was sent to the Girl Guides in a different uniform, medium blue with a leather belt and buckle. It wasn't quite as awful as the school uniform but to a Viennese child it was all very strange and humiliating. At fourteen I was already very much aware of my appearance. I had been given my first semi-high-heeled shoes that summer in Budapest, and secretly owned a pale lipstick.

Because of my limited knowledge of English, I was placed in a class with girls a year younger. Even so I could hardly follow the lessons, and I took to reading poetry under the desk and trying to translate some into German. It did not seem to worry anyone.

As I was utterly uninterested in sports and games, there were no points of contact. None of the girls were unfriendly but I was an exotic alien. I remember loathing hockey. Either I hit my shin with my own stick, or the hard ball I couldn't catch hit me, and I could never understand the rules. "Do we have to have Gitta on our side? We had her last time!" the captains used to cry, not unkindly, just desperate.

The English girls of thirteen in my class seemed younger than they would today, and infinitely younger than I was in 1938. My early enforced growing up was incomprehensible to them. The political situation in Europe, which in another year would lead their country into the Second World War, was as unknown to them as the yet unexplored moon. Whatever I could have told them about my life — apart from my language problem — would have seemed unbelievable exaggeration. Austria? Ah yes, that's where the kangaroos live! And Vienna is that place where they have canals instead of streets!

I started to isolate myself. Shakespeare's English was not all that strange — I had read a lot of his plays in German — and I loved English poetry, even when I did not understand it all.

The much maligned English cooking did not worry me. At fourteen one is always hungry anyway. Every Monday had its own strictly adhered-to menu for breakfast, lunch, and supper — and so did Tuesday and the other days of the week. On Sundays we all went to church, wearing special felt hats in the winter and straw hats in the summer, and gloves, no matter what the season. After church we met my hosts' friends and relatives, and they never tired of pointing out to me what good Christians my hosts were to have taken me in. I am sure I was the most ungrateful refugee child in Britain. Instead of being cheerful I sat in my room and cried, and nobody understood how desperately I was in need of warmth and affection. My hosts were very English indeed, and my behaviour very un-English. I longed for letters from Vienna; when they came, even though they were carefully coded, I sensed the increasing anxiety. Once a month a friend of my father's, the musicologist Emily Anderson, sent me one pound for pocket money. And that was a lot. Five English shillings a week at a time when nothing cost more than sixpence at Woolworth's! That first Christmas I bought presents for all eleven members of the household and still had money to spare.

Christmas — not the evening of the 24th, as I was used to, but the morning of the 25th — was a great occasion for giving presents. Each of the children had a large pile of gifts on his or her chair. And then there was a footstool and on it a navy blue school case and a bar of chocolate with a note saying "For Gitta." No embrace, no kiss. Only homesickness. On my birthday the following February I did get a kiss after all, and the *Albatross Book of English Verse,* never suspecting that twenty-one years later I would marry the former Albatross publisher.

After a mild English winter, spring came early and our south coast town seemed beautiful. The days grew longer, my English was quite fluent, and the strangeness seemed less strange. When the weather was fine, we were allowed to have certain lessons in the school garden, and I played Olivia in scenes from *Twelfth Night.* When it was warm enough, we swam in the sea, and the summer school uniform was a little less hideous than the winter version. I had made friends with two girls, one German and one Irish.

My father's letters still played down the situation in Vienna. Hitler and his Nazis seemed far away, and after all the regime could not possibly last! Even though I had not been allowed to go home for Christmas, surely it would be possible now, in the summer holidays? In the meantime my hosts had asked the Children's Refugee Committee to find me another home. I became an "After Care Case."

In June of 1939 my father was twice called before the Gestapo. They had found out who was behind a political article that had appeared in a Basle newspaper in March 1938. At the second interrogation the official said he could see no reason for not keeping him there. It was an unusual warning from such a source, and my father took the hint. The next day he asked the British Consulate to speed up the visa he had already applied for, and he was able to leave Vienna very hurriedly. It was high time. Three months later the war broke out and all the borders were closed.

He had intended to go on to America, the New York Public Library having offered him a job. His books had gone ahead in a large container. But first he moved to Cambridge, and when war was declared on 3 September 1939, he remained in England. His books spent the war years in New York harbour.

In the meantime, an understanding woman on

the Children's Committee had found me a new home in a village near Cambridge. I moved to the rectory of Little Shelford and was made welcome by a warmhearted rector and his family. It was a large unconventional household with cats and dogs and quite irregular meals. For a few weeks I was in a happy holiday mood. It was that unusually brilliant summer that Europe was granted before the war broke out on September 3rd. I still remember sitting under a tree in that rectory garden with pencil and paper, trying to write the story of my life. Those fifteen years had certainly been crammed with events, but in the end I had to admit that they would not fill a book.

My friendly hosts had previously volunteered to house evacuated London children if war broke out — and so I moved to a family in Cambridge. They proved real friends for many years to come. But now they too had committed themselves to take in London evacuees, and I had to move again. In my thirty-one years in England I moved twenty-three times!

In September there were still no signs of war. We were all given gas masks, and my father, OED, and I helped to fill sandbags that were placed around important buildings to protect them from shrapnel. We were still very naive about the meaning of war.

At that time I was staying in the same house as my father, with an interesting family of Italian origin. They had two children of about my age. Their rather conservative father had fought in the First World War in the same Italian region as OED, only on the opposite side. The two men took to each other in a big way, each in his more or less defective English. The mother, vivacious and generous, was a passionate communist. Among their paying — or unpaying — guests was a former director of Vienna's Albertina art museum; a Chinese student, later to become a tennis champion; a Basque and an English ex-Spanish-Civil-War soldier; two elderly English women; and an Italian university professor. I was sharing a small bedroom with the daughter of the house — which did not please either of us.

I was allowed another year at school, at the highly reputed Cambridge Perse School. I was to sit for what was then known as a "School Certificate," so that I would be able to get a job afterwards. Only slightly older refugees had no such opportunities. They could work only as domestic or hospital servants, or as farm workers. After the war started, this changed to some extent — many refugees could now replace Britons who were called up for military service.

I have always loved Cambridge, then and now. Those of us who were young, students or non-students, swam in or rowed and punted on the Cam. In the summer we lay in the grass, reading or talking, until late in the evenings. It was a peaceful, international atmosphere — as I knew it many years later when I worked for the United Nations in Vienna. At that time in Cambridge it was almost unreal. The war seemed far away in those early days. And Cambridge remained a peaceful oasis; it suffered only one bombing attack, even though there was a factory making precision instruments on its outskirts. OED and I had moved again, and this time I was given a room of my own and could put up my books and picture postcards of Vienna.

* * *

On 12 May 1940 my father was taken away by the police and interned. The year before tribunals had been set up for "enemy aliens," which we were, technically, with our inevitable German passports. People were divided into three categories: "A" meant suspicious, "B" uncertain, "C" reliable. Needless to say, these categories were not always correctly applied. When this tribunal was held in Cambridge, I was under sixteen and could therefore not be interrogated.

In the spring of 1940 Hitler's armies had invaded Holland, Belgium, and France. An invasion of Great Britain seemed imminent. At that point the British Government decided to intern the category "C" men and the category "B" women. The entire category "A" and the men of category "B" had already been interned at the outbreak of war. And then there was that small group who had turned sixteen after their local tribunals were held — not belonging to any category but now old enough to be interned. I was one of them.

When my father was arrested, neither he nor I knew where he was being taken. Two weeks later — I was still without news from him — they came to fetch me. When I returned from school on May 27th, a police car stood outside the house. Not in any unfriendly manner, but very matter of fact, a police woman told me to pack only as much as I could easily carry. I was not told where I was being taken nor how long I would be away. So I packed a rucksack — a number of books, a pair of shoes, some underwear, clothes and wash things. I was still in sandals, a summer dress, and cardigan, just as I had come back from school.

Together with women from Austria and Germany I spent the first night in the hall of a school, lying on the floor and using my rucksack as a pillow. In the morning we were taken to the station by bus. We still had no idea of where we were going. Because of the danger of an invasion, there were no longer name signs in the stations we passed through. Somebody mentioned we were going to Liverpool, and that proved to be correct. We spent the following night in an unused sailors' hostel, two or three of us to each cubicle. We slept on palliasses. An eighteen-year-old girl next to me cried all night — she thought she was pregnant and had not been able to say goodbye to her Canadian boyfriend.

On the third day we were taken to the docks — through the slums of Liverpool. The newspaper vendors were carrying placards reading GERMAN WOMEN, CARRYING TENNIS RACKETS AND SWIM SUITS, TO HOLIDAY ON THE ISLE OF MAN. We could not believe our eyes! The incited people pelted our buses with stones. A ship was waiting for us in the harbour. It was intended for a thousand passengers. We were four thousand.

Pregnant women and those with small children were given the available cabins. There was no milk for babies — one died in the night. None of us had eaten since we had left the sailors' hostel. We tried to find places where one could stretch out, on or underneath tables or benches. I lay down under a bench and read the *Oxford Book of German Verse.* It was already dark when the ship sailed, and in the morning we had our first sight of the Isle of Man with its fir trees and palm trees side by side. We were told that the islanders had their own currency and that their cats had no tails.

We were distributed in two adjoining small towns: Port Erin and Port St. Mary. Hotels and boarding houses had been cleared of carpets, curtains, and other "superfluous comforts." We looked after ourselves. Four of us young ones arranged to share a room containing two double beds. We were a strange assortment — a nurse from Cologne who was engaged to an Englishman, an Austrian countess who had been looking after children, and a Swabian farmer's daughter who had been visiting a sister married in England. But the vast majority of the women were refugees from Nazism, for racial or political reasons. Many had their children with them, as far as they were under the magical age of sixteen. Those over sixteen were internees in their own right!

It was May and the weather and the island were beautiful. But we had no news of our relatives and friends. There was no radio, no newspapers, so we lived on rumours. We formed friendships that outlived our internment by years.

In our boarding house I had to clean the stairs and later, when we had a camp post office, I was allowed to help sort the mail. Letters were of prime importance to us. My father and I were now able to correspond, on special, smooth prisoners' paper. But letters from one Isle of Man camp to another had to make the detour over the London censors — and that meant weeks of waiting. It had taken six weeks before we discovered that we were on the same island. Later he managed on one occasion to join a party of husbands who were allowed to visit their wives in our camp for a few hours. He just posed as my husband and nobody was any the wiser.

When I recall the horrors of Nazi concentration camps — and they already existed at that time — I am almost ashamed to write about our internment. Despite many bureaucratic and often superfluous harassments, we were never actually maltreated. That is true at least of the Isle of Man. But we were scared. We had no idea how imminent the danger of an invasion was. Most of us had fled from Hitler, and in the event of an invasion we would already have been behind barbed wire. At that time our worries may have seemed petty compared to the dangers facing the country, but the fate of Jewish refugees in France certainly proved us right.

At the beginning of August 1940 we learned of the sinking of the "Arandora Star." This one-time luxury cruiser was quite considerably over-loaded when it was hit by a German torpedo in the Atlantic. The majority of the internees it carried were of German, Austrian, and Italian origin. They did not stand a chance. Very few survived. A Viennese woman in our camp was informed that her husband had drowned. They had only recently married — both were Austrian refugees, she Jewish and he a Social Democrat.

A German friend of his had been able to save himself. He had the incredible presence of mind to take off his clothes except for a raincoat, jump off the boat and rub his body with the escaping machine oil from the sinking vessel. This and youthful resistance helped him to survive eight

hours in the icy Atlantic, hanging on to a board
of wood until Scottish fishermen rescued him.

Later I learned his dramatic story. Living in
Berlin, he was not allowed, as a non-Jew, to
marry his Jewish girl friend. She fled to England,
and shortly before the outbreak of war he followed her on a visitor's visa. When the war began,
he was of course highly suspect and was interned
immediately. I knew the girl in Cambridge. She
had tried to earn her living as a waitress. She
became very ill, and died during a cancer operation. With the help of other exiles I had collected
enough money for a rosebush to go on her grave.
After a number of articles published in the British
press and letters to Members of Parliament, we
succeeded in getting the man released and found
him work on a farm.

When we heard of the sinking of the "Arandora Star" that summer, none of us could know
for certain whether our friends or relatives had
been on the ship. The disaster was the first in-
dication we had that male internees were being
deported from Britain. Many of them were sent
to Canada, others to Australia. My cousin Stephan, who had survived the Dachau concentration
camp in 1938, was on the notorious boat "Du-

nera" which was bound for Australia. British soldiers, who could not differentiate between German prisoners of war and refugees maltreated many of them and robbed them of their few pieces of luggage. Some internees wanted to stay in those British colonies, but most of them preferred to return to Europe and fight against Hitler. Many of them planned to go home after the war in order to help rebuild their former countries.

My father was lucky enough to have a number of intellectual and artistic friends in his Isle of Man camp. They staged a very successful camp revue entitled "Oh What a Life!" OED wrote the words to a "Ballad of the Refugee" to music by the Austrian Hans Gál. It ended with this (very roughly translated) verse:

> Far removed from the great
>   events of the world,
> inactive in our war,
> our tied-up hands are raised to
>   the sky:
> oh Lord, let our warders win!

So that Old England's greatness
    be proved
in this struggle to free the world.
And when the bloody tyranny
    falls,
may our fate be decided as well.

We also had our artistic outlets in the women's camp: we staged scenes from *A Midsummer Night's Dream* in English — I played "The Wall" between Pyramus and Thisbe. I also recited poetry in English and in German. There were two actresses from Berlin I remember with great affection: one sang songs from Weill's *Threepenny Opera*, the other a humourous ditty in broad Berlin dialect. During my internment I once again planned to convert to the Jewish faith, as I had wished to do in 1938 — less from religious conviction than from a feeling of solidarity. But I was not serious enough to carry this through.

* * *

At the end of September I was summoned before a tribunal on the island. The interrogation began with the question: "Why did you leave Austria?" "Because of Hitler." "Why — what had Hitler done to you?" I burst into tears. It was an unnecessary cruelty. The authorities knew all about us and had detailed dossiers on every refugee. I was categorised as reliable at last, however, and was released at the beginning of October. My father volunteered to stay in his camp for an extra fortnight after his own release so that he could travel back to Cambridge with me. On a clear autumn morning we sailed to Liverpool as two free individuals. There we had our first experience of an air raid before we were able to continue our journey to Cambridge.

I had missed my School Certificate exams in July and had to prepare myself for the next date in December. I passed with good marks, but to this day I suspect that I was judged leniently because of my internment. Now the time had come, however, for the Children's Refugee Committee to insist — understandably — that I learn something practical so that I could support myself. I took shorthand and typing lessons, and while I never really became very skilled, I was able to earn my living. As long as no one is watching, I still type with only four fingers but with average speed.

In the meantime I had been moving again and again, from one family who happened to have a spare room to another. My father was now living in a university lodging house on a grant from the Society for the Protection of Science and Learning. The first version of his Schubert Thematic Catalogue — published in Britain in English in 1951 — was dedicated to the Society. With its secretary, Dr. Tess Simpson, I am still united in affectionate friendship. OED's English version of *Schubert. A Documentary Biography* bore the dedication "To Vienna's Past and Future."

After our return to Cambridge from the Isle of Man we joined a number of other ex-internees in forming a committee to help some of those who were still interned. We wrote applications to the authorities, and letters to the press and to the Parliamentary Committee for Internees. There were many Britons who were sympathetic to our plight and who understood that we — who had been refugees from Nazism — had every interest in supporting their fight against Hitler.

In Cambridge the "Free Austrian Movement" was organised in particular by the scientist Engelbert Broda. My father and I, always committed Austrians, supported the movement. It was important to explain to the British why an independent and democratic Austria would be an essential part of postwar Europe. We organised cultural and scientific events, and we younger ones — known as "Young Austria" — arranged English-language classes, outings, and theatricals. I still remember with affection a performance of James Bridie's *Tobias and the Angel* in the Cambridge Synagogue, with myself as the angel. There was a feeling of solidarity and optimism among us. In May 1988 a reunion was arranged in Vienna between those of us who had returned and those still living in Britain, with humourous and touching scenes between three hundred no longer "Young" Austrians.

I got my first job in October 1941, in the office of a very elegant store in Cambridge. The showroom floors were covered in thick lush carpeting. A pair of shoes there would have cost more than half my month's salary. Where the carpeting stopped, there was a curtain and behind it a wooden stair that led to a dark corridor and a long, narrow room — the office. There were eight of us, and in the middle of the room there was a small electric heater. The seating was arranged according to seniority. As the youngest I was furthest away from that heater and froze. Our working hours were eight-thirty to one, and two-fifteen to six. At ten o'clock we were allowed a break in an icy room where we were served a meat cube in hot water. The whole setup could have been used in any of Charles Dickens's novels. Thursday afternoons and Sundays were free. I was paid one pound twelve shillings and sixpence a week. At that time I was paying one pound ten shillings a week for my board and lodging.

My job was to enter the figures from the pay slips into an electrical counting device. No great task really, but given my disturbed relationship to figures, my mistakes were frequent. I also found it hard to be quite punctual, and we had to punch our cards in a time clock whenever we came or left. These cards were checked weekly, and offenders were summoned before the two directors and reprimanded — not too fiercely, I must add. Nevertheless I simply had to ask them for a rise, explaining my situation. It was a novel thought for them that a seventeen-year-old was not living at home with her parents, and they increased my weekly wage by two shillings and sixpence.

Among the many furnished rooms I inhabited during those years was one at the Vicarage of

Holy Trinity Church. I spent quite a few nights firewatching in the sacristy in order to guard the church against air raids. We were two girls and had no idea what to do in an emergency. The fact that the church is still standing today can only be attributed to the fact that Cambridge was spared serious bombing. When the sirens sounded, however, we put on our air-raid helmets, climbed on to the church roof and looked around. Climbing down again with an eery view of the moonlit churchyard below was pretty frightening.

But the peace of Cambridge did not reflect the situation of the country. From November 1940 onwards London and other big cities were heavily bombed. The civilian population reacted heroically, as indeed the British always do in dire emergencies. Most of the class arrogance that was so disturbing before the war, disappeared overnight. Quite a bit of it returned again later, but never to the extent that I had known before 1939.

* * *

The events of the war and the limited information about the atrocities of the Nazis in all parts of Europe reached us in Cambridge as if from another planet. But in other parts of Britain they knew about the war as thousands were killed in air raids, and whole towns, like Coventry, were completely destroyed.

The German and Austrian exiles lived in friendly unity based on a mixture of antifascism and homesickness. The homesickness of the Austrians was more pronounced, perhaps because they had lost their country more recently or maybe they were just more sentimental. Many of us intended to return after the war. Others swore never to return. These two schools of thought among the former refugees were to lead to differences and misunderstandings for many years to come. But for most of the second category Austria still became their favourite holiday choice — albeit often criticised.

As "enemy aliens" we had to adhere to certain police regulations. We had to be at home no later than ten in the evening, we needed permission to travel in Britain, and were not allowed to own cameras. With special permission one could own a bicycle, and that was important in Cambridge. It was taboo to speak German in public — a folly that could lead to unpleasantness. As a young girl I found the curfew hard, and so it happened occasionally that I was summoned to the Aliens

Office when I had offended against regulations. The police were friendly and knew most of us. There was an occasion when one of them stopped me on my bicycle after ten o'clock. Not only had I gone through the red traffic lights, but my bicycle lights were not working either. Trying to help me, he asked what serious reasons I had for this treble-offence urgency, and I explained that I was late for a party. On another occasion I had thoughtlessly lit an All Souls Day candle on the grave of my friend from Berlin who had died of cancer — forgetting that the cemetery was situated opposite a military airport. I managed to convince the police that I was not sending messages to enemy planes. Fortunately the police had our detailed dossiers and knew more about the refugees than about their own population.

One of the most touching and positive memories of the war years in Cambridge were the German services held regularly at the Chapel of Christ's College. Once a month they were conducted in two languages by the great and tolerant Dr. Bell, Bishop of Chichester, and young Pastor Hildebrand from Berlin, a friend of Pastor Niemöller whom the Nazis had persecuted. I spent a lot of time in church in those days, though honesty compels me to admit that the beautiful eyes of Pastor Hildebrand played an important part in my devotions.

I became a member of an idealistic amateur group of actors known initially as "The People's Theatre" and later as "Progressive Players." Although my English was now fluent, I still had enough of an accent to limit the parts I could play. But we performed with great dedication, sometimes at the Cambridge ADC Theatre, or at some village hall, or at a Royal Air Force camp — for which I obtained special police permission.

When we performed outside Cambridge, we hired a couple of coaches, one for the cast and one for costumes and what we used as scenery or props. The catering after the play varied according to the locale: instant coffee and rock cakes at the village halls and lovely steaks and chips at the Air Force camps.

Food and clothing were rationed, but we were used to that. We never went hungry, and, as far as I know, there was no black market to speak of. When available, fish and offal were on sale without ration books, and so were meals at restaurants or canteens — the only "rationing" concerned the amount you could spend there. My friends and I used to have lunch for a shilling at the "British

Restaurant." It wasn't exactly *haute cuisine* but it was adequate. The British prided themselves on their discipline. People helped each other as a matter of course, and queuing was accepted almost as a national pastime. Children and pregnant women always had sufficient milk, eggs, and orange juice — not to mention the perfectly foul cod-liver oil long before it was sold in capsules. The only "extra" we did not get used to was the occasional whale meat, probably because of the phoney assurance that it would taste exactly like steak if fried with sufficient onions.

In the winter of 1941–1942 I met the fiancé of my Berlin girl friend who had died so tragically. After his terrible experience on the "Arandora Star" he had been interned again and was finally released to work on a farm near Cambridge. His dramatic story had moved me deeply. I fell in love with him not only out of youthful romanticism but also because I wanted a family of my own. We married in 1942 and moved to London where he found another job doing "war work" at a uniform tailor's. We lived in a furnished room in St. John's Wood and spent most nights in air-raid shelters.

In February 1943 I moved to my friends, the

Oldfields, in Cambridge, and in March my daughter was born at Mill Road Hospital. My gyneacologist was an Austrian refugee and a monarchist, and when he announced that I had a lovely little girl, I told him that I would call her Elisabeth after the Empress of Austria. It was a white lie, for I had already chosen the name for other reasons. Elisabeth spent her early baby weeks in a flowering Cambridge garden, lying in a huge shabby pram which her grandfather had bought second- hand. I strictly adhered to the baby laws of Sir Truby King — and felt very grown up. Today's mothers will hardly believe that I fed my baby — in accordance with the book — exactly every four hours, with an undisturbed night's sleep from 10 p.m. to 6 a.m.

Once a week she was weighed and inspected at a baby clinic. She was a model baby in every way, even to the extent of modelling for a knitting pattern, wearing a bonnet and beaming at a rattle. It was the first money she earned — a guinea.

Pastor Hildebrand baptised her in Christ's College Chapel. When I pushed her pram along the street, an old lady enquired if I was taking my baby sister for a walk. I suppose I did look like a schoolgirl. The small difference in our ages later led my daughter to the spontaneous remark, "Do you remember when we were small . . . ?"

In the meantime my husband and I had found a flat in North West London, with a tiny bit of garden. The only furniture we owned was a double put-you-up, a kitchen cabinet with a flap-table, and two kitchen chairs. There was a cooker and a fridge and a fully equipped bathroom. Later my father bought us so-called "utility furniture" with his savings, just the bare essentials.

Not long after we moved, Hitler's unmanned "V-1" bombs began to fall on Britain. If the buzzing sound stopped a little distance away, it could hit us; if it stopped overhead, our house was safe. It was a nerve-racking time. Living on the ground floor, we were issued a "Morrison Shelter," a steel construction about the size of a double bed. If the house collapsed we stood a chance of surviving, provided we did not suffocate in the debris. As soon as the siren sounded, our neighbours from upstairs huddled in this contraption with the baby and us. Later, Hitler let loose his "V-2" bombs; they were soundless, and there was no warning. You were either lucky or you woke up in heaven.

By the end of 1944 our marriage had failed, and I moved to Cambridge with my little daughter and the cat. It was typical of my generous father that the words "I warned you!" never passed his lips. Elisabeth and I shared a furnished flat with a young Austrian girl. I found a job at the office of the Arts Theatre, and an all-day nursery for the child. But after a while I found the rent too high and was very grateful when the ever helpful Dr. Alice Roughton welcomed us into her large house, together with all her other lame ducks: students, land girls, and London evacuees. For a long time she had members of the German Ballet Jooss living there — famous for their anti-war ballet *The Green Table,* which had not endeared them to Hitler.

Thanks to Alice's generosity I could keep Elisabeth and myself on my small salary. It was an interesting life in this utterly unconventional household. A young woman looked after the various small children that Alice had taken in. Mine was the youngest. Apart from a frightening encounter with a large gander, she was happy enough. I came home in my lunch hour to make sure.

On Sunday evenings Alice held open house in the huge "Oak Room." Anyone could come and bring friends. And the most widely different people did in fact come to talk and to enjoy the friendly atmosphere. I remember a mild summer evening when a gentle horse walked in through the French windows, helped itself to a sandwich, and glided out again without causing particular comment.

At that time I formed friendships that have lasted to this day — with very dear Austrian twin sisters who belonged to the "Young Austria" circle, and with a young English woman, an actress in our amateur group, whose boy went to Elisabeth's nursery school. Work at the Arts Theatre was interesting, and I loved the friendly atmosphere among actors, stagehands, and the office staff. My usefulness seemed to be limited, and the manager described my nature as unsuited to an office. My personal life was very unsettled at that time, and I imagine my worries spilled over into my work.

The war was coming to an end, and in May 1945 Britain celebrated "Victory in Europe Day" — wildly on Trafalgar Square in London, a little less so in Cambridge, where we all went to see Lawrence Olivier as Henry V and cheered Shakespeare's patriotic words. It was "our" war too that had ended, "our" victory over Hitler. Austria seemed close once again. But we were afraid of

the news from there. Who would have survived?
What was left of Vienna, of Austria?

Gradually we received news from and about
members on my father's side of the family. One
of his sisters had been deported to Theresienstadt
concentration camp, three relatives had taken their
own lives, others had survived in hiding in Budapest. My brother Peter had been in a German
labour camp, and my Italian half-brother had returned to Trento from a British prisoner-of-war
camp in North Africa. My mother's relatives —
politically safe — did not have an easy time and
were now facing the tough awakening. My father
wrote a postcard to a musicologist friend in
Vienna in his typically laconic style: "It would be
nice to see you again." Anything had become possible once more.

* * *

In October 1945 my father managed to rent a
small furnished house in Cambridge. He lived in
the two downstairs rooms, and Elisabeth and I on
the first floor. We also had two lodgers: a young
Austrian girl, and a friend of mine who was book-
keeper at the Arts Theatre. I kept house for us all.
For a time I continued at the Arts Theatre, then
I worked freelance and part-time. I was also able

to do some library research for OED. His books had been returned from New York harbour, and he had new shelves built for them.

We had a small garden behind the house, and were within minutes of the river Cam. Elisabeth went to kindergarten, and I found time to read a great deal. Whatever I acquired in the way of education in those days I owe to the marvellous British public libraries. I later missed their size and quality when I returned to Vienna. There was little opportunity to listen to good music, but this may in part be blamed on my lack of interest. Only much later, back in Vienna, did I learn to appreciate operas and concerts.

I often had guests and tried to prepare Viennese food for them as best I could. OED would sometimes join us but most of the time he preferred to work. He was one of the most hardworking people I ever knew.

* * *

In the autumn of 1947 I had a few brief encounters with the philosopher Ludwig Wittgenstein. He needed someone to whom he could dictate in German, straight onto the typewriter. On the first day, he arrived with a paper bag full of vitamins

— at a time when we knew very little about them. "When you work with me, you will need vitamins," he said, and I obeyed without a murmur. He walked up and down in my living room and dictated incomprehensible words. At one point he paused and said, "I am an ass! But don't type that." I was told very much later that he had praised me greatly for "not asking silly questions." As though I would have dared! When I was no longer able to type for him, a Viennese friend of mine took over. She also claims not to have understood a word.

In 1948 I saw Vienna again for the first time since the war — a badly bombed, hungry Vienna, still occupied by the troops of the four Allies. And yet there was a sense of optimism. The roof of St. Stephen's Cathedral had collapsed in the final fighting. Yet, like a miracle, the old Gothic spire, the symbol of Vienna, had survived. The opera house and the Burgtheater were heaps of rubble. But the actors performed at the Ronacher Variety Theatre, and the singers sang at the Theater-an-der-Wien all the plays and operas that had been prohibited under Nazi rule.

From then on I interrupted my journeys to Vienna in Munich in order to stay with my mother's relatives and then spent a few days at the Salzburg Festivals. There were no charter flights in those days, and during the next twenty years I travelled by train and boat via Dover and Ostend — usually in the summer during school holidays.

* * *

My marriage was dissolved in 1948, and one year later I married an idealistic young Englishman who was studying English literature at Cambridge. He had been in Austria with the British occupation forces and had acted as an interpreter in Carinthia and in Vienna. On his return to Britain he was awarded a scholarship to Cambridge. We had practically no money but a lot of common interests.

At first we lived in a small furnished house in Cambridge. The bathtub was in the kitchen, the lavatory in the backyard. We were five: the three of us, a Nigerian student, and an English doctor — and of course Nitchevo, the cat. I used to bath little Elisabeth while our Nigerian friend cooked spicy meals. There was constant coming and going of students, with coffee and biscuits, and interesting discussions late at night. We were full of left-wing ideals and hopes of a better world.

Later we moved to a flat in South London with our own furniture bought from secondhand shops. My husband became a lecturer at London University, and Elisabeth went to one of the best and most modern primary schools in Dulwich. I found a job with a wine firm in Tooley Street. The Teltschers, refugees like myself, had been wine merchants in Nikolsburg, the little Moravian town my grandparents came from. It was this fact that earned me an extra ten shillings each pay-day, very discreetly pushed into my hand while no one was looking. More than forty years passed before I saw Nikolsburg for the first time — and in the overgrown Jewish cemetery there were as many Deutschs as Teltschers. My time in Tooley Street was an education in itself. Between London Bridge and Tower Bridge, the workers had a code of decency and solidarity. In our lunch hour we would listen to the lay speakers by Tower Bridge — their language every bit as lusty as that of their rivals in Hyde Park. In the afternoon one of us would go out to buy penny "doorsteps" — thick slices of bread and dripping, covered in onions. At Christmas the firm would book a table at the nearest pub, and we would eat a traditional Christmas dinner, office and cellar staff side by side.

* * *

The further you turn back the pages of your memories, the easier it is to write about them. Later events are far more difficult to describe and are subject to one's own censorship. In the course of time we tend to suppress some of the darker sides of life, but also ungratefully forget its bright and positive sides.

My generation hardly knew what it was to be young. We had to switch from childhood to being adults without any transition. In my case it all happened in such a short span of time. My mother died when I was thirteen. One year later Hitler's troops occupied Austria, and I was sent to England. The following year the war broke out, and eight months later I was interned. Yet one year later I was working and keeping myself. Another year went by, and I married at the age of eighteen and had my daughter when I was nineteen. One year later this first marriage had failed. Yet all this could not be compared to what some of my contemporaries went through during that time.

The Austrian refugees made great efforts to convince the British Government that it was essential for Austria to become a free and democratic state, and independent from Germany. That was not always easy. Of course there were many Britons who appreciated our situation. But there were others who saw no difference between Austrians and Germans and anyhow considered that the only good German was a dead German.

Many Austrians who felt politically involved wanted to return as soon as the war was over to share in the rebuilding of Austria. It required a great deal of conviction and idealism because very few were asked to return. My father and I always knew that we would go back one day. Our feeling was that not even those seven years of Hitlerism could change the long history of our country. But other exiles swore never again to return.

When my father went back to Austria in 1952, it was easy enough for me to understand his decision. My daughter, who had been born and educated in England, found it far more difficult to accept my return to Austria seventeen years later. But for the time being the question did not arise for me. Elisabeth was still at school, and I was married to an Englishman. But the frontiers were open, and I could travel to Austria, to visit old friends and make new ones.

My father rented two furnished rooms in Vienna and continued to work. He had brought his books and book shelves with him from England. Our flat in Böcklin Street was of course gone and the furniture sold. He used to go to a cheap restaurant across the street for lunch, and in the evenings read the daily papers over a dish of scrambled eggs and a glass of milk at the Café Imperial. We wrote to each other every week, and OED's letters — sometimes no more than half a closely typed page — were succinct but brimming over with interesting news about himself and cultural life in Vienna.

During the Festivals he was always in Salzburg and would hold court over a second breakfast at the Café Basar, surrounded by young and old musicians and musicologists. After a night's journey from Ostend, I would drop my luggage at a hotel and then go to find him there. He would look up for a moment, give me one of his charming smiles and say: "I seem to know this lady!" Behind this cool and reserved air lay great affection. We were well attuned to each other.

When we could afford it, my husband, my daughter, and I loved to spend part of our summer holidays in Austria, partly in Vienna, and partly at some lake.

The year 1953 saw the coronation of Britain's young Queen Elizabeth. The whole of London was decorated. Britons not only love their historic pageants, they are also very good at them. Very few people owned television sets in those days, but the coronation was televised. Coronation festivities took place at every British school, and it so happened that one evening on my way home from the office I opened a newspaper and saw once again a child dressed up as Elizabeth I. The face under the wig seemed vaguely familiar, and on closer inspection turned out to be that of my nine-year-old daughter looking down on a young Sir Walter Raleigh with haughty dignity.

That same year I spent a week in Budapest as a translator at an International Peace Congress. Our British team was repeatedly approached in the streets by royalty-hungry Hungarians who wanted coins or postage stamps with a picture of the new queen.

During those years I frequently travelled to Trento in Italy to visit my half-brother and his family. Despite my lack of Italian and the family's limited German, I felt very affectionately accepted. Later Elisabeth accompanied me and she spent some happy summer holidays with them all on the island of Elba, returning with fluent Italian.

In May 1955 Austria was at last granted its State Treaty, signed by the foreign ministers of the four Allies: Great Britain, France, the Soviet Union, and the United States. Austria committed herself to a status of permanent neutrality. In his letters my father told me how moved he was by this solemn event which seemed to bring about the fulfillment of both our wishes. Austria was given special treatment. Unlike Germany, she was described as Hitler's first victim. Today I am no longer convinced that this decision was fair.

The four armies of occupation left Austria that same year. For ten years Austria — and Vienna separately — had been divided into four zones. And at a time when the Cold War was already firmly established, you could still see the famous jeep driving through the centre of Vienna — one French, one British, one Soviet, and one American officer, side by side.

In 1955 the Opera House and the Burgtheater were rebuilt, and in the autumn historical opening performances took place in both houses. Many Viennese queued day and night for tickets. My father was invited to both first nights. A few weeks later, on one of my visits to Vienna, I was lucky enough to see one of the first performances of Beethoven's *Fidelio*, and of Schiller's *Don Carlos*. The atmosphere was overwhelming — a blend of enthusiasm and deep emotion — among the artists as well as in the audience.

* * *

In the meantime sadly my second marriage had failed. We parted amicably, and Elisabeth and I lived alone once more. Despite a mutual exchange of children arranged with other mothers, particularly during school holidays, it proved easier for me now to work for a secretarial agency. It enabled me to take time off when necessary, albeit without pay.

Through one of my job assignments I met a fascinating man who would have fitted better into the eighteenth century than the twentieth. He was cultivated, sophisticated, self-willed, and charming — and twenty-seven years older than I. In the thirties he had published the first paperback in the shape we have all grown accustomed to. His English language Albatross books were beautifully produced on the Continent of Europe and could only be sold there. The firm no longer existed at the time we met, but he was still very active in a number of spheres, travelled a great deal, and found my bilingual secretarial abilities useful.

A few years later we married. He had rented the Norman Keep of Chilham Castle in Kent — a twelfth-century fortress — and spent a lot of money on making it habitable. Each light switch needed special permission from the Ancient Monuments Authority. He had a lift built, a kitchen and two bathrooms. The building consists of an octagon and an irregular rectangle. The dining room took up two floors of the octagon, above it was the living room. The rectangular part had three levels: the kitchen, my bedroom, and that of my husband. The flint walls of the building are about six feet thick, and they retain the dampness of eight Kentish centuries. The lead window frames seemed only arbitrarily to fit the small panes; on the other hand, there was a useful hole under one of my windows for pouring boiling oil on potential intruders! The building was difficult to heat. To get it really warm would have ruined us financially. It was the original castle of Chilham and it was beautiful. From its roof we had the most romantic view across the gentle landscape of the Kentish hills. It is said that a greedy bishop was granted a request by King John, and promptly asked for all the land that could be seen from the roof of Chilham

Keep. He certainly didn't get it!

The present and actual Chilham Castle stands next to the Keep, and was built by Inigo Jones at the beginning of the seventeenth century. The park with its large lake was laid out by the famous landscape gardener "Capability Brown" in the eighteenth century. There is a "ha-ha," separating sheep and horses from the rest of the gardens, an avenue of Spanish chestnuts, three very old mulberry trees, and a windless rose garden surrounded by a wisteria-covered wall. I believe they all date back to Capability Brown. Chilham Park is known to have the largest and oldest settlement of herons, with more than a hundred nests. It was first mentioned in a chronicle of 1280. Quite inexplicably — but confirmed over and over again — the herons return to their nests from the south each year on the 14th of February, St. Valentine's Day.

* * *

Elisabeth had moved to Kent with me in 1959, and that entailed exchanging her sympathetic London school for one in Canterbury that she liked far less. She decided to leave that school as soon as possible, a decision I should have perhaps opposed. She wanted to become a nurse, a training she could only begin at eighteen.

A wonderful friend of both my husband and my father, whose friendship and affection is a central theme in all our lives, invited Elisabeth to his family in Luxemburg for this interim before she could start her hospital training. She was welcomed into a cultivated atmosphere, where she learned languages, enjoyed good music, and was able to pass her driving test. She also met, in the family's eldest son, her future husband.

But then she returned to Kent and took up her three years' very strenuous nurses training at Canterbury Hospital. She had the reputation of taking great and very personal care of her patients, particularly those for whom there was no hope. She was terribly upset at every death she witnessed. I am quite convinced that the only good nurse is one who can feel deeply and yet stay the course. She did, and she received her diploma as State Registered Nurse.

In 1964 many scenes from the film *Moll Flanders* with Kim Novak were shot at Chilham Castle, in and around the lake, and in the village square. The villagers were asked to take part as extras in a market scene. Elisabeth and I also reported early one morning to be handed our costumes. One look at Elisabeth produced a beautiful crinoline dress and matching hat. One look at me raised the comment, "Ah yes, a fishwife." Although the particular scene was finally cut, there is a photo of a haughty Elisabeth inspecting the grey rubber fish lying on my stand. But there are a few brief seconds where she can be seen standing on one side of a horse, with our landlord, the owner of the castle, on the other. The film company had to find lodgings for most of their crew in the village. The general opinion in Chilham was that there had been no such excitement since the new drains were installed.

On one of the few occasions when my husband took the initiative for making easy money, we offered to let the Keep to Kim Novak and her charming dresser, a black American with the unlikely name of Blanche. We moved into our guest flat at the castle. The film company's publicity manager told journalists that the ghost of King John had sat on Kim Novak's bed. He had never visited us, but you can see his point of view when you think of the lovely Kim.

In December 1965 my daughter married the young man she had met in Luxemburg. My husband and I had grown very fond of him. It was a mild day, so Elisabeth could walk across the park and the village square to Chilham Church, just wearing the white velvet dress she had made herself.

The "children" usually came from London to spend the weekend at Chilham. It was a harmonious, interesting, and stimulating time, but also a time when we already worried about my husband's health and when financial problems loomed ahead.

The year 1963 saw the beginning of the Stour Music Festival, so called after the Kentish river Stour. It had been founded by the counter-tenor Alfred Deller and the Royal Academician John Ward. My husband advised on financial questions.

The most beautiful concerts of early music were performed in the fairy-tale setting of Olantigh House, which belonged to a cultivated couple who for many years lent the house to the Festival in June. Nikolaus and Alice Harnoncourt, with their *Concentus Musicus,* were guests of the Festival on two occasions, long before they were as fully appreciated in Austria.

The river Stour runs through Olantigh park, with its wonderful flowers and statues. The combination of a traditional English country house and music of outstanding quality belongs to the unforgettable memories of my life. To begin with, there were the three of us, and after Elisabeth married we were four, attending most of the concerts. Elisabeth and I used to volunteer to help with the cold buffet — usually salmon and cucumber, followed by strawberries and cream, as befits an English June.

After my husband died, I was invited to spend a private weekend at Olantigh, and that was the only time in my life that the scent of roses outside my window was strong enough to wake me in the morning.

Alfred Deller is no longer with us, but his son Mark continues to run the Festival and my children have long ago joined the regular supporters. Olantigh is no longer available, but many of the concerts take place in the old village church of Boughton Aluph. My granddaughter Juliet has become a professional singer, and is now taking part in the Stour Music concerts — so the family link has moved on to the third generation.

But to return to December 1966 when Juliet was born. I have tried faithfully not to think of her as my second daughter. It has not always been easy. She and her mother still occasionally drift

through my dreams in the shape of a fair-haired
little girl, and on waking I wonder which of the
two it was. At weekends I was allowed to have the
baby in my bedroom. She was an enchanting,
self-willed little creature. For a very long time she
could not be bothered to talk although she
seemed to understand every word. One day she
looked up at an embroidery hanging above my
bed, and calmly said "butterflies and flowers," as
though that was the easiest thing in the world.

* * *

My father had become very frail and in need of
care. He spent the last two years of his life in a
sanatorium in Baden near Vienna, where his
friends and relatives visited him faithfully and
regularly. He told me that when he was a little
boy, there used to be an inn where the sanatorium now stands, and that he recalled being
knocked down by a horse and cart and waking up
in the innkeepers' bed.

On my visits to Vienna, I used to spend the
afternoons with him in Baden. We would walk
arm in arm along the corridor from one window
overlooking the ruin of castle Rauhenstein to the
opposite window overlooking the ruin of castle

Rauheneck. On fine days he would let me take him to the garden in a wheelchair and, having arrived there, say very firmly "And now turn me round so that I don't have to look at these old people!" After all, he was only in his early eighties!

I now used to travel to Vienna four times a year, moving between worries about a sick husband and worries about a sick father. Quite apart from the family ties in both countries, I was so emotionally involved with Vienna that on my return journeys I was usually in tears before the train reached the next station. It is said that cats are more attached to places than to people. Perhaps my great affinity with cats accounts for some of this.

In October of 1967 I saw OED for the last time. I had always made a point of turning on the television news before saying goodbye, to divert him. In his utterly unsentimental way but unmistakably, he simply said, "Ah well, dear Gitta. . . ." I knew and he knew that it might be the last time. He died a few weeks later, at the end of November, with a snapshot of his great-granddaughter Juliet — whom he had never met — on his bedside table. Until the very end he kept talking — half wistfully, half ironically — about

the "bibliography of his still unwritten books."
But life had ceased to interest him since he could
not work any longer.

During a very moving memorial ceremony the
actor Fred Liewehr was kind enough to read the
poem "Abendlied" by Mathias Claudius, and the
violinist Eduard Melkus and his students played
the adagio from Schubert's only string quintet, as
OED himself had suggested in his Last Will.

My husband had come to Vienna the day before and suffered a severe stroke during the night.
He recovered only very slowly and never completely, and in March 1969 he died of a heart
attack.

I then decided that the time had come for me
to return to Vienna. My husband, through no
fault of his own, had died in debt, but I was pre-
pared for the situation. A week after his death I
was given six months' notice to leave the Keep.
The "children" helped me with the enormous task
of winding up and preparing my move. In May I
went to Vienna to find a flat and to apply for a
job with UNIDO (United Nations Industrial Development Organisation).

* * *

At the end of July 1969 I moved to Vienna — to temporary accommodation, putting my furniture in storage. I had already found a small permanent flat in May, but it was not vacant yet. It overlooked Vienna's largest market, the Naschmarkt, opposite the historically famous Theater-an-der-Wien. Then I took Juliet for a lakeside holiday while her parents had a holiday in Yugoslavia.

Early in September I passed my shorthand and typing test and started work with UNIDO on 16 September. On that day I met the best friend I would have in the organisation. She is one-quarter Swedish and three-quarters Spanish, and had joined UNIDO at the very beginning, in 1967. My first boss was of Russian-Jewish origin and Advisor to the Executive Director — who was an Egyptian. This constellation symbolised for me the spirit of the United Nations. In those early days UNIDO was small enough for people to know each other. When we moved to the huge skyscrapers on the other side of the Danube, the Vienna International Centre, the increased number of staff, the other organisations, and the uniformity of our offices made cooperation and personal contacts far more difficult.

I worked with UNIDO for fifteen years,

almost without promotion but with the enrichment of many international friendships. If the United Nations had achieved nothing else — and to say so would indeed be unfair — but the bringing together of so many different nationalities, political systems, colours and religions, it would in my eyes have achieved a great deal. Industrial development as such was of less interest to me than the general idea of the United Nations, including the work for peace and for the emancipation of women.

Apart from the separation from my family, I enjoyed these early days in Vienna. I earned quite a lot of money by my standards and had some very good friends. Some I had "inherited" from my father, some came from the world of theatre and literature, others were new UNIDO friends.

I came to know the new Vienna, the new Austria. And I learned German again — an unofficial "advanced course." Not only had the language changed considerably since the thirties, but the vocabulary of a fourteen-year-old needed bringing up to date.

Outside my working time, I had endless possibilities — theatre, opera, concerts — I had so much to catch up on. Vienna's wonderful swimming baths, the ease of getting out of town and to its green surroundings, weekends in the country. Everything was new, experiences and impressions. Perhaps I discovered Vienna "for the first time" in the same way as my international colleagues. I just had the advantage of knowing the language.

Moving our office from the centre to the new buildings brought some disadvantages — from the impersonal atmosphere of so many identical floors to the much disliked air-conditioning. But we had the most wonderful views from our curved triangular skyscrapers — the Vienna hills, Kahlenberg, Leopoldsberg and Bisamberg from one side, the many-armed waters of the *Old Danube* from another, and in the winter a colourful Breughel-like picture of children skating on a lake from the third side.

In summer we used our lunch breaks to walk through the large parks to the *Old Danube* bathing places for a short swim or, after office hours, for a longer one, lazing under tall old trees. When the first underground line was built, the journey from the opera house to the Vienna International Centre took only twelve minutes. In the summer holidays I was able to take Juliet to the Austrian lakes or to the Salzburg Festivals and the "Carinthian Summer." I shall always remember her enthusiastic reaction to Bernstein conducting his *Kaddish Symphony* with the Israel Philharmonic in Villach!

When my flat above the market became vacant in December 1969, I had it renovated and moved there in January. It was the first time in my life I had signed a lease. I had brought what furniture I needed for two rooms from Chilham and was now able to arrange things according to my own taste. Only the market separates me from Theater-an-der-Wien, I can look into its foyer from my living-room window. The market has always been a joy, the many nationalities among both vendors and buyers, the inland and the exotic fruit and vegetables, the farmers' market on Saturday mornings, and in the winter the colourful Advent garlands on the florists' side. I can walk to the opera house in a few minutes.

The son of good friends, a qualified carpenter, came to discuss with me — sitting on the bare floor with apple juice and frankfurters — what could be done with my limited amount of money. All the built-in furniture was made by him. He was very young and proud of his work, and when his father helped me to put up my books, he decided the shelves had looked far better without them. I arranged the furniture I had brought from England, I could even use some old curtains. For the first time in Vienna I began to invite guests. Forty people came to my house-warming party. Somehow they managed to find the space in two rooms and a kitchen. Later I reduced that figure but I did on occasion still have up to twenty guests.

One of my best friends in Vienna was the musicologist Christa Landon. She had acted as a "spare daughter" to OED while I was still living in England and could only come for visits. I often stayed with her. Her flat was the hub of musicians and musicologists from abroad, and I met the most interesting people there, and many future friends. Her kitchen suppers are among my happiest memories of those years. Two motherly women played an important part in my new life — both were artists. One was the actress who became my "confirmation godmother," the other a pianist, painter, and sculptor, both old family friends.

At Easter 1972 my half-brother died in a car accident on the motorway between Innsbruck and Bolzano, through no fault of his. We had become very fond of each other. It was a terrible blow to his family in Trento. They never really recovered from the loss. In the course of time the younger generation in particular became friends. Whereas my sister-in- law and I still converse with the help of dictionaries on the few occasions we meet, her children speak English, and the younger members of the family in Britain speak Italian.

My brother Peter and his family had been living in Vienna since the fifties, and here too there is a son and a daughter. With them and their children I also have affectionate relations.

* * *

In the winter of 1974 I spent six days with a dear friend in New York. On the outward flight I read a paperback edition of Gerhard Fritsch's poems entitled *Der Geisterkrug* and on the return flight started to translate some of these poems into English. I "filed and polished" these for a few years until I was lucky enough to meet Anthony Rudolf of The Menard Press, who published them in London in 1978.

On another journey to the United States seventeen years later, I once again translated poetry on the plane from New York to Vienna — this time, my own.

But to return to the seventies: In the autumn of 1977 I spent a holiday in Israel with a friend before I had to undergo an operation in Vienna. A few days later, on November 19th — the anniversary of Schubert's death — Christa Landon was killed in a plane crash over Madeira. She, Arnold Feil, and Walther Dürr were the pioneers of the New Schubert Edition, produced in Tübingen and Vienna and published by Bärenreiter in Kassel. It is a work of decades, and younger musicologists have joined the team since then.

In the late seventies I met the scientist Engelbert Broda again at the home of friends. My father and I had known him in Cambridge as long ago as 1941, and we both thought highly of him. He returned to Vienna in 1947 and after some years became Professor of Physical Chemistry at the very university institute where he had studied as a young man. He later became chairman of the Austrian branch of the *Pugwash Movement,* an organisation of scientists — founded by Bertrand Russell and Albert Einstein — against nuclear warfare.

Pugwash is a small fishing village in Nova Scotia. A generous Canadian financed and arranged the first conference there. A very moving story about this important movement is little known:

Bertrand Russell had obtained Einstein's agreement to sign the manifesto with him. On a plane between New York and Paris, Russell heard the news of Einstein's death. It thus seemed that this all-important partner was lost to the cause. When Russell reached his hotel, however, there was a letter from Einstein, with the signed manifesto.

My next years were greatly influenced by Engelbert Broda. We travelled to places that only he knew, and others that were new to us both. But above all he showed me Austria because he loved the country and had always been an enthusiastic walker and mountaineer. As I could not claim to be either, we found ways and means to compromise.

As he had been involved in early nuclear research he was well-qualified to speak about the subject, and he became a firm opponent of Austria's production of nuclear energy. Before a plebiscite was held in respect of the atomic power station at Zwentendorf, he spoke against its use on radio and television, and his power of persuasion was considerable.

Bert Broda was a quite exceptional man, one

of the few who lead their lives according to their own moral code. He was also infinitely kind, very humourous, and the most reliable of friends. His sudden death on 26 October 1983 — Austria's National Holiday — evoked a feeling of permanent loss not only in myself. Contrary to the usual trite phrase that everybody is replaceable it can be said that he remained irreplaceable.

The following May, at a peace demonstration in Vienna, students hung up a huge banner with the words ENGELBERT BRODA UNIVERSITÄT between the pillars of the university's main entrance. In the street where he had lived there were plaques reading ENGELBERT BRODA STRASSE. The students had loved him. He was known to be willing to listen and to make allowances for the opinions of others. No matter how great the pressure of his work, he would always make time for discussions, with the cleaners at the institute every bit as seriously as with his students and colleagues. He was asked to speak on nuclear disarmament to many religious and political organisations in Austria and abroad.

Every year he brought the statistics of nuclear arms arsenals up to date. One of his great hopes was the development of solar energy for its inexhaustibility as much as for its lack of military potential. He much regretted the insufficiency of funds for world-wide research.

A personal anecdote helps to show the sort of man he was. We were sitting in a little restaurant garden when he began to get worried. Two little boys in the park were wildly shaking the branches of a tree and then picking up some nuts. I could see his dilemma. The environmentalist in him was concerned for the tree. The philanthropist and children's friend in him, on the other hand, could not possibly scold these boys who were obviously immigrant children and probably not treated too well by the Viennese anyhow. He walked over to them and tried to explain the problem of the tree. They were friendly and offered him some of their nuts. He tried again, and this time they understood. Then he asked them to wait, rushed back to the restaurant, bought two large ice-cream cones, and rushed back to the boys, pushing the cones into their respective left hands and heartily shaking their respective right hands. After that he returned to our table with a deep sigh of relief.

Through Bert Broda I also met Peter Smolka, editor of the excellent quarterly *Austria Today*. He not only encouraged me, but also gave me the chance to translate poetry and short stories and to write articles and book reviews for this magazine.

* * *

I retired from the United Nations in 1984 and started to write at long last — poetry at first, then reminiscences of my life which, inevitably in this century, have become contemporary history.

In 1985 I was awarded the first Wystan-Hugh-Auden Prize for Poetry Translation. Utta Roy-Seifert, who had founded the Austrian Translators' Union, had encouraged me to compete, and she acted as the main speaker at the award ceremony.

I first discovered the poetry of the Austrian writer Erich Fried through Bert Broda who had known him in the days of their British exile. When Bert died, we sent out hundreds of announcements, and I included a poem which Bert had always carried with him and had copied endless times for his friends and students. I realised too late that I should of course have asked for Fried's permission, so I wrote to him and apologised. His reply was generous and warm-hearted, and he suggested that we should meet on his next visit to Vienna. It was a strange feeling

when, after Erich's death, I was given a postcard
from Bert addressed to Fried, on which he also
apologised for having copied and frequently
handed out this very same poem!

When I finally met Erich Fried, he already
knew that he had incurable cancer. During the
next few years I was privileged sometimes to
accompany him to his readings or his visits to the
hospital. I greatly admired not only his poetry but
also his courageous fight for time. He travelled
and read his poetry and prose in all parts of
Europe till the day he died.

I had written a small cycle of love poems after
the death of Bert Broda, and the writer and critic
Hans Weigel presented them at the Austrian
Society of Literature — together with the poems
of three "other young" unknown poets! I owe the
publication of these poems in 1988 to the help
and encouragement of Erich Fried. He found a
young publisher in Salzburg, and wrote an after-
word to the book.

With the support of the Austrian Cultural
Institute in London, I read at the German departments of five British universities in February 1989
— poetry by Erich Fried, Gerhard Fritsch, and
Christine Busta, as well as some of my own
poetry and prose.

The summer and autumn of 1989 were of course marked by the exciting events in Eastern Europe that seemed to develop so quickly in, as we thought, the best possible way — a euphoria we soon had to abandon.

In the same autumn I was found to have cancer. After the first incredulity and shock, I was petrified. And then, with a feeling of angry determination, I decided to put up a fight. I knew quite a number of people who had survived cancer. One doctor, a relative of Bert Broda's, patiently explained the situation to me. So far, only the "secondaries" had been found — but they were plentiful. I was sent to a young oncologist and after meeting him I felt that there was hope. He found the "primary," a small lump in my breast. To make sure, he wanted further tests, but his first diagnosis had been correct. After a breast operation, we were relieved: the carcinoma was of the same substance as the "secondaries." A dear friend looked after me for nine days, while the oncologist worked out a "tailor-made" programme of chemotherapy. It was a gentle therapy spread over six months. I spent four days in hospital with infusions, then four at home with a course of tablets, then again four days in hospital, and sixteen at home with tablets. While I was hanging on the drip for hours on end, I flatly refused to read anything on the subject of cancer. I decided on a light diet consisting mainly of John Mortimer's *Rumpole of the Old Bailey* and P. G. Wodehouse. Every evening the oncologist would come to see that all was going well. He was always positive, humourous, and relaxed — the latter an outstanding talent in a terribly hard-working doctor. He used to sit by my hospital bed as though he had all the time in the world and no other cancer patients. My trust in him was infinite. It was like walking through fire and through water with him — as in Mozart's *Magic Flute*. I was lucky to have no problems with my blood tests, therefore no therapy dates needed to be postponed.

I knew that chemotherapy meant losing one's hair — the poison that splits the cancer cells also splits the roots of your hair. I had mine cut very short on the basis that short hairs on my pillow would upset me less than long hairs. I also bought a really glamorous wig. And again I was lucky: I did lose my hair but without going completely bald.

On my days at home I led a full and normal life. I went to the theatre, to concerts, to the opera, met my friends for meals, or went swimming. At the beginning of each four-day period a friend took me to the hospital; at the end of the four days, her brother brought me home. The feeling of being cut off from the rest of the world soon left me. Whatever I needed was provided by wonderful Indian nursing nuns, and the support and affection of my friends was like a pillar of strength.

The 8th of June 1990 was my last day at the hospital. It was summer, and I went swimming every day at my favorite bathing place by the *Old Danube.* My hair began to grow, better and stronger than before — one of the odd consolations after chemotherapy.

A reading tour I had planned for the United States in April 1990 had to be called off, but I was able to arrange it for the following spring. I was invited to read at the German departments of four American universities. I travelled from New York to St. Louis, Missouri, then to Boston and Connecticut. It was a very impressive fortnight with warmhearted hospitality. I found the students as interested and willing to talk as those in Britain two years before.

* * *

With advancing age the years seem to reel off with increasing speed. And my life, which had not always seemed worthwhile, has become far more precious. Growing older brings certain advantages. Adjustment to other people's opinions can be eliminated. I enjoy the great luxury of organising my own time and making my own decisions. I would even claim that you can still fall in love — without being misunderstood. As far as love is concerned, I took a long time to mature. Although my reasons were not the same as his, I could say with Othello: ". . . then must you speak of one that lov'd not wisely but too well . . ."

Of course I am also afraid of aging, like most people, afraid of "having to watch it happen," as the Feldmarschallin says in Richard Strauss's *Rosenkavalier.* But I have never cheated about my age and have learned to face both mirrors and X-rays.

Of course I am afraid of loneliness, afraid that backaches will increase and hamper my getting out of bed in the mornings. Even though there is such a thing as a telephone and at the other end some friend who has my keys, things that function today may become problematic tomorrow.

Of course I am afraid of change, afraid that my kind and efficient weekly help will one day give up looking after my flat, and afraid of becoming a burden to others.

Inevitably the ranks of older friends and contemporaries are thinning out. There is only one really sure method of avoiding the threat of a lonely old age, and that is to turn around and stretch out both hands to the young and the very young — so that the bridges may hold between the generations.

Many of my contemporaries have an irrational but not unusual feeling of guilt at having survived the Nazi terror. Now I have an added feeling of irrational guilt: why should I survive cancer and so many others die?

My life still holds a great deal of pleasure — bathing in the soft, natural water of the *Old Danube,* looking at the surrounding hills, or lying on wooden planks under the old poplars. Or spending a week at my favourite small lake in southern Carinthia, with its dramatic backdrop of high mountains. Theatres and concerts, carefully chosen television programmes and, last but by no means least, the telephone, that vital link with people who need me and people I need.

I have immense trust in the present-day young. In 1984 I joined some of them in their endeavour to save one of the last and irretrievable riverside forests to the east of Vienna. It would have pleased Engelbert Broda who, a few years earlier, had fought for the preservation of the most beautiful historic stretch of the Danube further up, the Wachau. He had written to all the mayors of the region, urging them to form a committee to prevent the building of a hydro-electric power station right in front of Dürnstein Castle, where England's Richard the Lionhearted was said to have been imprisoned. Broda received the Austrian Award for Nature Conservation for his initiative.

The young will be responsible for the future of our vulnerable blue planet of which it is rightly said that we have only borrowed it from our children. Time and again it is possible, particularly in Austria, by means of plebiscites and demonstrations, to avoid errors or to reverse erroneous decisions.

The riverside forests along the Danube, with their unique but threatened flora and fauna, have not been ruined, nor has the Wachau.

When I returned from my British exile in 1969, I thought everything in Austria was wonderful. This traditionally antisemitic country had a Jewish Federal Chancellor and a Socialist government. I am not quite as blue-eyed as I was then. But there have been remarkable changes. The Waldheim affair brought about an Austrian version of *glasnost*. Although a lot of unsavoury events and attitudes emerged, a great many people protested against his candidature. There were round-the-clock demonstrations outside St. Stephen's Cathedral, and flowers and candles where the "O5" sign had been cut into the wall by the resistance fighters. The sign stands for "Austria": O and the fifth letter in the alphabet reads OE = Oesterreich. For many weeks on Sundays we silently walked from St. Stephen's to the Presidential Residence, with banners protesting against Waldheim, even after he was installed as president. His highly simplified autobiography read: "I was wounded as a soldier in Russia in 1941 and then returned to my studies in Vienna." Then, gradually, he had to admit what he was doing between 1941 and 1945. He was too young to be a war criminal, but he was an intelligence officer in one of the most notorious divisions of Hitler's army, very close to Saloniki when all the Jews were deported from there, and very close indeed

to villages that were wiped out in former Yugoslavia. An international commission of historians
was asked to investigate, and they confirmed that
he could not have helped knowing about those
atrocities. Even then, Waldheim lacked the grace
to resign, claiming that he had been elected by an
"overwhelming majority." It was not all that
overwhelming in fact, but a lot of Austrians had
been angered by outside interference.

There are a number of things that happened
at that time and are worth mentioning. In the
middle of the Waldheim controversy, for instance,
a group of young people were waiting outside
Vienna's main synagogue one Friday evening,
with flowers and banners of solidarity with the
congregation.

I remember visiting an exhibition at Vienna's
Historic Museum about the notorious *Reichskristallnacht* pogrom. There was a class of school
children, fourteen or fifteen years old, who were
looking at the terrible photos. In the middle of
the exhibition hall three old park benches had
been placed, one of them still bearing the white
printed words NUR FÜR ARIER (For Aryans Only),
as a memorial of those days. When the youngsters
had been round the exhibition, they collapsed in

youthful exhaustion on two of those benches. Not on the third. That remained empty.

Alfred Hrdlicka's artistically controversial sculptures entitled "Memorial against War and Fascism" were erected just behind the opera house. The prostrate figure of the humiliated old Jew is often covered with flowers or branches.

These days I am often astonished how much more easily people talk to each other on controversial subjects. "I am Jewish or of Jewish origin" is no longer whispered apologetically. Others speak quite openly about their Nazi families and how the knowledge had weighed upon them. It has become far easier, of course, to speak of Nazi grandparents or even great-grandparents than to feel the need to defend your own parents' politics.

There is much to criticise in Austria, and a great deal to praise. Racialism, supported by certain newspapers, and the so-called "Freedom Party" with its extreme right-wing leader Jörg Haider, stands in opposition to a politically decent radio and television and quite a record of humanitarian activities. When an earthquake destroyed much of Armenia, the Austrians built a village there, with a school and health centre, entirely from private donations. In the Kurdish refugee camps the Austrians established two hospitals with Austrian doctors and nurses. And those are just two of many similar activities involving mainly young people.

On 21 June 1991 — it was the first day of summer, warm and sunny — I was at Feldkirch in Vorarlberg at one of the *Schubertiade* concerts. I had just heard the news that Jörg Haider had tripped up on one of his pro-Nazi statements and was at last dropped as head of the Carinthian provincial government as a result — and that Waldheim had decided not to stand for re-election.

That evening I had a feeling that the Austrians carried their heads a few centimetres higher. Naivety perhaps, or my incorrigible optimism. But the opposite of optimism would be capitulation.

A lot of things have happened since then to shake this optimism. Racism and antisemitism rear their ugly heads from time to time. Gravestones were broken up in the old Jewish part of our largest cemetery. It cost me quite an effort a few days later to visit my grandparents' grave. I did not know what to expect, but their grave was untouched. Some art students were sketching the broken gravestones to see what could be repaired by the municipality.

Shortly afterwards, ten thousand Viennese took part in a silent walk to protest against anti-semitism — in pouring rain.

Time and again there are manifestations of human decency. On 21 July 1992 fifty to sixty thousand mainly young people arranged an open-air concert to demonstrate against xenophobia. Late at night Eli Wiesel, Auschwitz survivor and Nobel Peace Prize winner, spoke from the very balcony on the Heldenplatz where Hitler had held his notorious Anschluss speech in March 1938.

Since then a cruel war is raging in former Yugoslavia. Things we no longer thought possible in post-war Europe are reaching us daily through the news. Austria started a campaign entitled "Neighbour in Need," organised on a completely non-profit basis by Austria's broadcasting company, the Red Cross, and the Catholic Caritas. Already in the first seven weeks private and public donations had amounted to three hundred million Austrian Schillings, thus providing the first thousand lorries carrying food, medical and sanitary supplies, and baby food, to the refugee camps and the people in Bosnia. Since then, these figures have multiplied many times over, and this humanitarian service still continues.

On 23 January 1993 we were a quarter of a million people silently walking to the Heldenplatz from all parts of Vienna, carrying torches and candles. A lot of young people in groups, or with prams, small children carrying Chinese lanterns. It was a demonstration for tolerance and humanity — an ocean of lights, as far as the eye could see.

And this is Austria too.

ILLUSTRATIONS

Great-grandparents: Dr. Adolf and Sophie Richter

Maternal grandparents: Wilhelm Müller, nee Richter,
with their four children. Standing: Hanna

Paternal grandparens: Ernestine Deutsch, nee Gewitsch,
and Ignaz Deutsch

Father, Otto Erich Deutsch, 1910

Mother, Hanna Deutsch, nee Müller
left: as Red Cross nurse during the
First World War

Hanna and Otto Erich Deutsch, shortly after
their marriage in 1917

Gitta, 1928

As *"Jackie Coogan," 1929*

With her brothers Peter and Erico Deutsch,
in Syria, 1932

Neuenbürg in the Black Forest, 1935

Villa Talwiese, Reichenau an der Rax

Wittelsbach-School, Towards Rotunden-Bridge

The last class photo , 1938. Front row:
Lotte fourth from the right, Gitta fourth from the left

As "Cyclamen" in a children's play,
at Vienna's Kammerspiele-Theatre, 1935

Otto Erich Deutsch in the 'thirties

Vienna 1938 (Photograph by Robert Haas)

With daughter Elisabeth, Cambridge 1943

Elisabeth and Gitta as extras for the film
"Moll Flanders," 1964

Otto Erich Deutsch, Vienna 1955

Mallorca, 1956

The Keep and Chilham Castle

The "children": Elisabeth and Konrad, 1985
Grand daughter Juliet, 1990

With Engelbert Broda, Styria, September 1983